THE ELECTRONIC DOPPELGÄNGER

The Mystery of the Double in the Age of the Internet

RUDOLF STEINER

Edited and Introduced by Andreas Neider

Translated from German by Simon Luke Breslaw

RUDOLF STEINER PRESS

Rudolf Steiner Press,
Hillside House, The Square
Forest Row, RH18 5ES

www.rudolfsteinerpress.com

Published by Rudolf Steiner Press 2016

Originally published in German under the title *Der elektronische Doppelgänger* by Rudolf Steiner Verlag, Basel, in 2013

A catalogue record for this book is available from the British Library

Print book ISBN: 978 1 85584 525 1
Ebook ISBN: 978 1 85584 477 3

Cover by Morgan Creative
Typeset by DP Photosetting, Neath, West Glamorgan
Printed and bound by 4Edge Ltd., Essex

CONTENTS

A Note on the Translation

The German term *der Doppelgänger* (literally, a 'double-goer') has been translated throughout as 'the doppelgänger' rather than as 'the Double'. This is partly because 'doppelgänger' (or 'doppelganger') is used in English, but also because it is an apt choice of translation in the context of online social media phenomena, such as digital avatars (see the Introduction and Afterword by Andreas Neider). It avoids conveying the misleading sense of a psychological alter ego and, for that reason, seems appropriate in the light of the distinction made by Rudolf Steiner between the ahrimanic doppelgänger, who only accompanies us for a single incarnation, and the luciferic doppelgänger (or Double), as mentioned in the Introduction.

Simon Luke Breslaw

INTRODUCTION

by Andreas Neider

In the lectures of November 1917 gathered here in abridged form, a topic emerges that Rudolf Steiner only spoke about in these particular lectures, or more precisely, in the lecture held in St Gallen on 16 November and in the lectures held in Dornach on 18, 19 and 25 November 1917. Neither before nor after did he speak about the secret of what he called the 'geographical doppelgänger' or the 'ahrimanic doppelgänger'. The reason why we have entitled this volume 'The Electronic Doppelgänger' will be explained in more detail below.

First, however, Steiner discusses several other topics (both in the St Gallen lecture and in the Dornach lectures), which all relate to the topic of the doppelgänger, as we shall see. He first speaks of the existence of western occult brotherhoods that have an interest in propagating materialism to such an extent that ever greater numbers of the deceased are thereby unable to extricate themselves from earthly existence. For souls that remain entangled within the material realm after death produce destructive effects, which these brotherhoods are able to make use of for their own purposes.

Connected with this is a first main theme of these lectures, namely the interests of certain western occult groups who are seeking to control the Earth by material and technological means, and whose activities extend into the realm of the dead. According to Steiner, this exercise of power is only possible because certain secrets are kept secret and deliberately withheld. These secrets relate to the supersensible nature of the human being and concern the 'ahrimanic' or 'geographical' doppelgänger.

By speaking about these previously undisclosed occult facts for the first and only time here in these lectures, Rudolf Steiner deliberately counters this principle of maintaining secrecy in order to exercise power. For that reason, these lectures are of huge significance in terms of the secrets revealed within them, as will be explained in what follows.

Before doing so, however, we need to consider the historical background to the matters set out here. This concerns what Steiner refers to as the 'fall of the spirits of darkness'. He had previously spoken about that topic in the lectures held from the middle to the end of October 1917 in Dornach,[1] and again, shortly afterwards, in Zurich on 6 and 13 November (the relevant passages have been included in our compilation).

The 'fall of the spirits of darkness' relates to these matters as follows. Steiner described a historical but supersensible event that took place between 1841 and 1879 as a kind of reflection of the fight with the dragon described in the Apocalypse. In order to prepare for his rulership as the Time Spirit from 1879 onwards, the Archangel Michael (who is also referred to in the Apocalypse) had to cast out the spirits of darkness onto Earth, i.e. into the consciousness of human beings.

This battle in the etheric world ended after 38 years in 1879. Michael had triumphed over the spirits of darkness, who, since that time, can only operate in the physical world, i.e. within the earthly consciousness of human beings. And 38 years after 1879, the earthly consequences of this fall were manifested in 1917. This explains why Steiner spoke about the matters discussed here in the year 1917 in particular. He also characterized materialism, which had been spreading since the 1840s, as the ultimate expression of this fall.

We now have to consider what type of spirits Rudolf Steiner means when he speaks about the spirits of darkness, whom he characterizes as belonging to the realm of the Angeloi. In particular, we need to consider the kind of consciousness the Angeloi possess. As angels do not have physical bodies but etheric bodies as the lowest constituents of their being, they live in their thinking directly in the etheric sphere, thus without needing to reflect their thoughts in a physical body. In the etheric world, the 'time here becomes space' dictum applies. Everything that in the physical world must be thought in temporal succession appears *simultaneously* in the etheric.

In their thinking, angels therefore live permanently in this space or 'anti-space' of the etheric. Thoughts do not arise in succession for them but are simultaneous and permanently observable as a kind of panorama. Furthermore, angels do not need their etheric bodies to maintain a physical body and can therefore fully dedicate all their energies to the activity of thinking. As a consequence, angels possess foresight and a clairvoyant overview (which is also what enables the personal, guardian angel, who accompanies a human being, to guide that person's destiny).

At the beginning of the modern period, a whole grouping of angels had turned to Ahriman, thereby darkening and obscuring the etheric sphere. This is what Michael, the ruler of this etheric thought sphere, had to redress by casting out these beings into the earthly realm. Angels that become 'spirits of darkness' and are cast out of the etheric into the earthly realm, the realm of human consciousness, lose their previous clairvoyance in the process. They are cast out of the etheric web of light and panoramic vista of simultaneity into our earthly consciousness, where succession in time is determined by physical materiality. This kind of darkening or obfuscation is one of the essential characteristics of the being whom Rudolf Steiner calls Ahriman. Ahriman wishes to bind the consciousness of human beings, their free powers of attention, to the earthly realm. With the help of the spirits of darkness, he seeks to obscure the etheric from human beings.

This is a goal that Ahriman has only been able to achieve since the time when thinking effectively took up its seat within the physical body. Before the dawn of the modern period, human beings did not think with their physical brains, but with their etheric bodies. That meant their thoughts were not as closely tied to the nerve-sense system as they are today. Since the onset of the modern period, however, thoughts are reflected in the physical body. Thus bound to the nerve-sense system, living ideas are paralysed as we experience them, and this is what enables us to research and understand material processes with such precision.[2] Living thinking that is woven within the etheric is limited in a sense by the physical body and deadened.

The further evolution of human consciousness should now consist of us overcoming the darkening linked to materialistic consciousness by our awakening to the etheric quality of thinking. However, that is precisely what the spirits of darkness, those Angeloi beings, are seeking to prevent, since, due to their ahrimanic colouring, they had to leave the etheric realm and can now only operate within the earthly realm of our materialistic consciousness.

Knowledge of this historic occult event was another secret those western brotherhoods wished to keep to themselves, so as to be able to exert power. Rudolf Steiner also spoke about this, again entirely deliberately in 1917, in order to make knowledge of these matters accessible to humanity. For if the powers of the 'spirits of darkness' were used in such a way that nobody else could have any knowledge of them, then that would naturally be the best way of fixating human consciousness on the purely material, even after death.[3] It is only against this background that the real focus of the lectures gathered here, the secret of the 'geographical doppelgänger', can be understood correctly.

In these lectures of the autumn of 1917, Rudolf Steiner calls attention to a particular feature of our nervous system. He explains here, for the first and only time, that there is a being within our nervous system that does not belong to what constitutes the human being at all—an ahrimanic being that enters the human being shortly before birth and is forced to leave again on the latter's death. This ahrimanic being provides a basis for all the electrical currents we need in our nervous system in order to process our sense perceptions, coordinate them and react to them.

> The human being thus arrives into this world with his organism in which he clothes himself, without reaching down into this organism with his soul. There is, however, an opportunity, shortly before we are born (not long at all before we are born) for another spiritual being, in addition to our soul, to take ownership of our physical body, of the subconscious part of our body. It is just a fact that, shortly before we are born, we are permeated by another being, whom, in our current terminology, we would call an ahrimanic spiritual being. This being is as much within us as our own soul is within us. Such beings

> live their lives by using the human being in order to be present within the sphere in which they wish to be. They have an extraordinarily high level of intelligence and a very highly developed will, but nothing in the nature of a life of feeling [*Gemüt*], not what we would call a human life of feeling. And so it is indeed the case that we go through our lives with a soul and this doppelgänger, who is cleverer, far cleverer than we are. This being is highly intelligent, but possesses a Mephistophelean intelligence, an ahrimanic intelligence, as well as a very strong will, a will that is much closer to the forces of nature than our human will, which is tempered by our life of feeling.
>
> In the nineteenth century, natural science discovered that the nervous system is permeated by electrical forces—and natural science was right about that. However, if science holds, or scientists believe, that our nerve forces, which belong to us and provide a basis for our life of thought, have anything to do with electrical currents passing through our nerves, then they are mistaken. For the electrical currents are the forces that are placed into our being by that other being, whom I have just described, and do not belong to our being at all; we do also carry electrical currents within us, but they are of a purely ahrimanic nature.[4]

Medical science tells us that electrical currents, so-called action potentials, are built up and transmitted both in our brain and within the rest of our nervous system. These are measurable with an ECG or EEG. If a current flows, then this is a message that is transmitted, which triggers the relevant chemical reaction; if no current flows, then this is also a message, and no chemical reaction takes place.

Our entire nervous system is pervaded by such currents, which convey stimuli to the brain that are received via sense organs from the outer world. They also coordinate, via the nerve pathways and nerve cells, the movements of our muscular apparatus in response to sensory stimuli. For example, if the surface of our hand conveys a strong stimulus from a hotplate, our arm reacts instantly and our hand is immediately retracted. This reaction requires neither a thought process nor an emotional response. The soul remains completely excluded in this case, while the body reacts with a spontaneous reflex.

The ahrimanic being who lives with us in our body is therefore necessary for our earthly consciousness. We would not be able to live without this being, which is also apparent from the fact that our life ends the moment no electrical current flows through our nervous system.

At the same time, however, Rudolf Steiner also identifies this ahrimanic doppelgänger as the originator of illnesses—specifically, illnesses that depend upon geographical conditions. Why is that? It is because the ahrimanic doppelgänger is himself subject to geographical conditions, since the Earth is also permeated by electromagnetic forces. These forces are aligned according to the Earth's mountain ranges and are particularly strong where mountain chains run from south to north, rather than from east to west. Rudolf Steiner points out that these forces active within the human nervous system correspond to such electrical and magnetic forces. He then indicates that humanity in the twentieth century will be in a position to transfer these forces to machines.

> I have frequently pointed out, quite deliberately, including in public lectures,[5] that human consciousness

> is associated with forces of destruction. [...] into our nervous system we die. These forces, these death forces, will become ever more powerful. *And the connection will be made between the death forces in the human being, which are related to electromagnetic forces, and outer machine forces. In a sense, the human being will be able to let his thoughts flow into the machine forces.* As yet undiscovered forces within the human being will be discovered, forces that have an effect on outer electrical and magnetic forces.[6]

Now, one of the pioneers of computer technology in America, John von Neumann, described his method of developing the computer in the 1950s as follows:

> To design the machine, my co-workers and I tried to imitate some of the known operations of the live brain. This aspect led me to study neurology [...] and, eventually, to give lectures on the possibilities of copying an extremely simplified model of the living brain for man-made machines.[7]

As the only one among his colleagues, von Neumann studied neurology alongside his work on developing the first computers. That is why no one apart from him noticed what they were actually doing in developing these machines. Transmission of all information in the computer, just as in the nervous system, is based on the polarity of current/no current. In the case of the human organism, however, a significant amount of chemistry also plays a role (in terms of what are known as messenger substances or neurotransmitters). When we consider computer technology, it is apparent from the above that we are dealing with an externalized ahrimanic doppelgänger, whom, in the context of the lectures by Steiner gathered here, I would like to call the 'electronic doppelgänger'. It is no accident that, for a long time now, the computer has been called the PC, the personal computer. Almost all the work we do with our minds is now done only with the help of computers and their networking via the internet. Nearly all areas of our life—our personal data, our work, our consumer purchases—are captured and recorded by computers. The 'personal' computer does indeed now accompany us as a kind of electronic doppelgänger.

And the nature of the personal computer is exactly as Rudolf Steiner described the ahrimanic doppelgänger:

> And so it is indeed the case that we go through our lives with a soul and this doppelgänger, who is cleverer, far cleverer than we are. This being is highly intelligent, but possesses a Mephistophelean intelligence, an ahrimanic intelligence, as well as a very strong will, a will that is much closer to the forces of nature than our human will, which is tempered by our life of feeling.[8]

The computer is a cold machine with a very high level of intelligence and an uncompromising will, otherwise known as efficiency. Numerous processes of movement, including the conduct of warfare, are today guided by computers. Even our economic life, with all its money flows, is today largely controlled by these machines.

It is therefore evident that Rudolf Steiner had such an extensive overview of the technological developments of the twentieth century that he was able to foresee the transition from the industrial age to the digital age.

At this point we should discuss the term 'doppelgänger'. Steiner used this term in all his basic works, in his lectures and in his Mystery Dramas to designate a being who accompanies us like a shadow, even after death and through our different lives on Earth. At a certain point in the lecture of 16 November 1917 (reprinted in this book) he distinguishes the 'ahrimanic' doppelgänger discussed here from the 'luciferic' doppelgänger, whom he otherwise simply refers to as the doppelgänger [or 'the Double'], in the sense of the human being's shadow. The distinction is essential, in so far as the ahrimanic doppelgänger only accompanies us from birth to death during one life on Earth.[9]

In this lecture, however, Steiner goes one step further by connecting the discovery of the ahrimanic doppelgänger with the previously described 'fall of the spirits of darkness'. He describes the attempt by western occult lodges to keep these facts secret in order to exploit them as a deliberate means of exerting power and of darkening people's awareness of supersensible reality.

In order to understand this connection, we have to look more closely at the physiological basis of human soul life. We have a nervous system that supports our sense-bound consciousness. The latter is not identical to our soul experience. In order to become aware of a sense impression, we require a sense organ and the relevant nerve pathways in the brain and nervous system. The nerve impulses generated can be physically measured and observed—but not so our soul experience! The colour red and the song of a blackbird will never be found physically in the brain or in the nerve pathways. Where then does this soul experience occur, if it cannot be found within the body?

The answer to that question is that our soul experience does not take place in the body but where the sensory phenomenon is located, i.e. outside of the body. After all, I do not hear the blackbird singing in my head but on the branch of a tree. I do not see the colour red in my eye, but externally on the wall. In our soul life, we are always with the things that we are perceiving at that moment.[10]

The nerve-sense organization merely serves as a kind of mirror in which we are able to become conscious of our soul experience, as Steiner had described at an earlier date.[11] But how does the soul experience outside the body relate to the nerve-sense organization? Rudolf Steiner spent almost his whole life researching the gap that opens up here between the realm of the soul and the physical/bodily realm.[12] He sought to understand the link between the soul and the body right down to the physiological details. In doing so, he discovered the essential function of the etheric body.

To begin with, the function of our etheric body is to animate, construct and organize our physical body.[13] It is the designer who shapes the organs and regulates their interactions. However, these forces of form and organization are not only used to animate and organize physical materials but can also be used to grasp, shape and retain experiences gained through our soul-spiritual faculties (i.e. through our 'I' and our astral body) in the form of thoughts and perceptions. Our memory enables us to bring our soul experiences to life again repeatedly.

Steiner pointed out on many occasions, as one of his central discoveries, that the nature of our etheric body undergoes a change around our seventh year of life. After the formation and construction of the physical body has been concluded, a part of the life functions of the etheric body is freed up during the second seven-year period and can henceforth serve the creation of thoughts and memory. Our powers of thought and memory, we could also say our powers of attention, are therefore transformed life forces. They could also be called 'free forces', as they have been 'freed' from the task of providing for the life of our physical body.

> At the beginning of a human earthly life (most noticeably during the embryo period), these forces within our etheric body act as forces of creation and growth. During the course of earthly life, a part of these forces emancipate themselves from their formation and growth activities and become the powers of thought that bring about the shadowy thought world for normal consciousness.
>
> It is of utmost importance to know that the normal powers of thought of the human being are in fact refined forces of formation and growth.[14]

How, precisely, does this transformation take place, which becomes outwardly apparent from around the age seven onwards?[15] In the inner part of the brain there are ventricles, which are a network of blood vessels (choroid plexus). Here, arterial blood, which supplies and maintains life, is converted into cerebrospinal fluid. Our brain and central nervous system are kept almost afloat within this fluid, while the fluid itself is constantly moved by the rhythm of our breathing. It rises and sinks within the spinal canal, depending on whether we are breathing in or breathing out.

In this physiological phenomenon, we have an accurate reflection of the transformation of the formative life forces (which find their expression within the arterial blood) into the powers that shape our experiences. These are the 'free forces', which, freed from the metabolic process, are manifested as the crystal clear cerebrospinal fluid.

Our astral body lives within our breathing. Through our breathing in and breathing out, our astral body is able to influence the cerebrospinal fluid because the rhythm of our breathing is transferred via our diaphragm to the fluid flowing within the spinal cord.

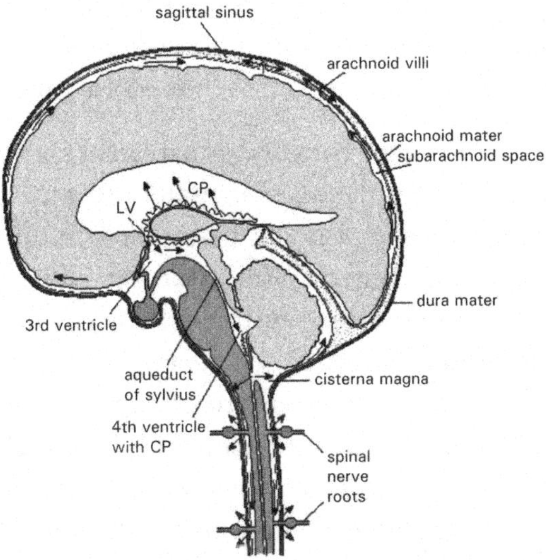

Fig. 1: Schematic illustration of the brain with the flows of cerebrospinal fluid indicated by the black arrows. The checkered area (choroid plexus) shown with the arrows pointing upwards in the inner part represents the network of blood vessels, in which the inner cerebrospinal fluid is formed. This flows out via the two ventricles shown bottom left and right. The inner grey surfaces should be imagined as permeated through and through by the plexus of nerves, which is then linked via the nerve tracts to the sense organs. (Source: A. Husemann, *Der hörende Mensch und die Wirklichkeit der Musik* [*Human Hearing and the Reality of Music*, translated and published in English by Rudolf Steiner Press], p. 74.)

The astral body is thereby able to draw on the formative forces of the etheric body (that are no longer required for the metabolic process) for its own purposes. From a physiological point of view, this forms the basis of our mental images and our feeling life.

> Our ability to form images of the outer world derives from the fact that the rhythm of our breathing touches upon our nerve currents. Thoughts, abstract thoughts, are still entirely bound to the nervous system, but the visual element is linked to our living breath. Therefore, you could say: here we have life as a formative force.[16]

The astral body of the consciously experiencing human being requires for the formation of consciousness, i.e. the formation of mental images, a bodily basis that is able to emulate or reflect these experiences. While our nervous system forms the basis for our dead, abstract thoughts and imageless concepts lacking in feeling, our living thinking and experiencing are related to the cerebrospinal fluid that is brought into oscillation through our breathing.[17] The soul experience of the astral body finds a connection to the material/physical processes in the nervous system via the rhythmic breathing in the cerebrospinal spinal fluid, which is the former arterial blood now freed from the metabolic process. The same sculpting, formative forces of the etheric body (which previously built up the physical body by transferring nutrients within the arterial blood and supplying them to the vital organs) are free to be used from about the seventh year onwards, as was already mentioned, in the formation of conscious and deliberate mental images.

If human beings only had an astral body and an 'I' but no etheric body, then, although they would be able to have experiences and sense impressions, these would be fleeting, and it would not be possible to retain them. The etheric body is also what retains our experiences until their dissolution, which is when they are let go by the astral body, i.e. when they are forgotten. Through the venous blood, the etheric body is able to hold on to experiences in such a way that they are imprinted like the characters of a script into the various organs and, in connection with them, into the brain. These processes are therefore also what underlies the formation of memory.

As the formative forces are not transformed back into forces that form and nourish the body, but remain in a sense available as 'free forces', they are able to imprint material representations of the content of mental images into the body. In this process, the relevant parts of the brain form the material basis.

When the astral body relinquishes the formative forces, i.e. if a mental image or soul experience fades from our consciousness, then, in its place, a purely etheric form is created that is no longer held in our consciousness. Physiologically, this corresponds to the reabsorption of the cerebrospinal fluid into the venous blood. In this manner, the etheric body changes from being the 'preserver' of the physical body to the 'preserver' of the contents of consciousness. In the remembering process, these stored memory contents are then 'read' by the astral body within the etheric body as past experiences.

The soul reads the signs imprinted into the physical body in the same way that we hear music via the physically resounding notes, even though the essence of the music lies in the spirit realm between the notes. It reads them in the same way that we read letters on a page, even though the content of what is written does not live on the page. In this way, the soul recalls past experiences that are represented in the bodily engrams.

However, the 'inscribing of engrams' does not happen

immediately, as it normally takes three days and nights until what has been experienced has actually been processed by the etheric and physical bodies. This processing mainly takes place during the night. Our dreams are a manifestation of this nightly remembering, since they arise on our awakening through the astral body and the 'I' coming into contact with the etheric and physical bodies.[18] While we consciously attend to our experiences and sense impressions, our etheric body continuously works on incorporating and imprinting them into our physical body.

We have now outlined a subject area that we need to be familiar with in order to understand the technology related to the 'ahrimanic doppelgänger'. The powers of remembering and creating mental imagery actually reside in the etheric body. However, not only are they bound to the nervous system, such as is the case for dead abstract thinking and mental picturing, but also, as Rudolf Steiner said in the passage quoted above:

> These forces, these death forces, will become ever more powerful. And the connection will be made between the death forces in the human being, which are related to electromagnetic forces, and outer machine forces. In a sense, the human being will be able to let his thoughts flow into the machine forces.[19]

But this means nothing other than that the technology foreseen by Steiner will no longer be industrial technology but *consciousness technology* or, more precisely, *attentiveness technology*. This technology breaks the connection between the nerve-sense system and our soul/spirit precisely at the point where the two are connected via the free forces of the etheric body, and replaces the 'free forces' with the electronic doppelgänger! Our soul experience, including the creation of memory, is thereby bound to the machine. Or, to put it another way, a large proportion of humanity's powers of attention are now bound to machines with the help of the consciousness technologies of the internet and computers. Many of our memory functions are also being replaced by the computer and the internet, the latter in the sense of a universal, albeit virtual, technical medium.

When we use the internet, do we not get the impression that we are thereby connected to the world? Are not many parents worried they would exclude their children from the rest of the world if they were to keep them away from Facebook? And does it not appear as if we can connect to a kind of universal human memory via the internet and Wikipedia?

This is exactly what Rudolf Steiner predicted in the lectures gathered here. He then also describes how these technologies, originating in America, will spread throughout the world.

> Those who will seek to introduce the Antichrist as the Christ are attempting to exploit what is able to act through the most material of forces but which, in actual fact, acts in a spiritual way through the most material of forces. Above all, this group is seeking to exploit electricity and the Earth's magnetism in order to generate effects throughout the world.[20]

Steiner thus makes it clear that, in connection with the fall of the spirits of darkness, an attempt will be made to absorb the development of the free, etheric forces of our consciousness. This is because the spirits of darkness had to leave the etheric realm and therefore have an ever greater interest in keeping human consciousness away from this sphere. At present, they achieve this primarily through those machines that imitate consciousness processes within the human organism, processes that are bound to the senses and based on electrical currents, and ultimately, therefore, based on the ahrimanic doppelgänger.

However, and this is now crucial, Steiner views the creation of new machines, machines that he believes humanity will increasingly merge with, as something that is unavoidable.

> In these places, the will is there to yoke the power of human beings to the power of machines. Matters such as this must not be treated as if they needed to be opposed. That would be a completely false view. For these things will not fail to materialize, they will come about. What is important is whether they are introduced into the course of world history by human beings who have selfless knowledge of the great goals of earthly evolution. The issue is whether those who introduce these things do so for the salvation of humanity or whether they are brought onto the scene by groups of human beings who only exploit these things for egotistical or group-egotistical purposes. It is not what is coming that matters in this case, as what is coming is coming for certain; it is how these things are dealt with that matters. What is coming is simply what is in accordance with the Earth's evolution. The forging together of human nature with the nature of the machine will be a significant problem for the rest of the Earth's evolution.[21]

It is precisely in this respect that Rudolf Steiner attempts to develop a future spirit consciousness. In the last days of his life, he formulated his well-known Leading Thoughts on the relationship between sub-nature and super-nature:

> Human beings must find the strength, the inner strength of knowledge, in order not to be overwhelmed by Ahriman in our technological civilization. They must understand sub-nature for what it is. Human beings can only do so if they have climbed at least as high into extra-terrestrial super-nature with spiritual knowledge as they have descended with their technological knowledge into sub-nature. The current age requires an understanding that *transcends* nature, because, inwardly, it has to come to terms with the dangerous effects of the purpose it has assigned to life, which has sunk beneath the level of nature. Of course, the point is not to advocate a return to earlier cultural conditions, but for human beings to find a way of bringing the new cultural conditions into a correct relationship with themselves and with the cosmos.[22]

And that is why he warned that these consciousness and attentiveness technologies would be exploited in a one-sided way in the aforementioned interests of western occultism, so as to spread darkness over everything spiritual.

What was important to Steiner in these lectures was to show how the future soul-spiritual evolution of human beings will increasingly take place within the context of a confrontation and coming to terms with new technologies. These technologies seek to bind our consciousness to the machine and to the realm of sub-nature. It was therefore important to Steiner that we have a clear understanding of the power that ahrimanic beings have within the new consciousness technologies. For although they are in essence consciousness technologies, their one-sided use, without an understanding of their effects, will have consequences for our own consciousness. For this reason, Steiner speaks in this context of human beings increasingly becoming what they think themselves to be.

We must take hold of the free powers of attention of our etheric body. We must grasp our powers of memory through our soul-spiritual natures and not allow them to be ruled by the world of machines. Viewed against this background, the exercises that Steiner gave to develop our powers of attention (via concentration, meditation and the nightly review exercise) have an almost life-determining importance for the future.[23] As human beings, we will only remain equal to the challenges of technological civilization if we can counter those forces that are attempting to usurp our powers of attention by means of the electronic doppelgänger. We will only be able to counter them with a decisive strengthening of our powers of attention through our awakening to the etheric sphere. Above all, this means we must become familiar with the etheric nature of our powers of attention, in order that we may use them consciously. That was the aim of all the exercises that Rudolf Steiner gave in this regard.

Our becoming conscious of the nature of our own being is what mattered to Steiner. By alerting us in the following lectures to the ahrimanic doppelgänger, he indicated at the same time the realm where human beings will remain tied to the purely earthly/material, if they do not learn to rise above it. The technological evolution described in these lectures has brought with it the danger that human beings will increasingly be tied to the earthly, material realm as a result of the displacement of the ahrimanic doppelgänger into the machine world through the creation of the electronic doppelgänger.

In this context, Steiner indicated that, by strengthening our own thinking, by training our powers of attention, we train our ability to perceive supersensible realities. At the same time, we develop our ability to enter into a relationship with the world of the dead, a relationship that is no longer tied to physical, material existence, but one that belongs in the etheric world, the realm of our powers of attention.

If, as Steiner indicated in these lectures, human beings in the future will increasingly become what they think themselves to be, then, by becoming conscious of our own supersensible being, we will also create the power to free ourselves from our ties to the earthly realm after death, and thereby develop an awareness of the supersensible facts of life after death. In this respect, these lectures are also a wakening call for the spiritual activity of each individual human being.

THE 'ELECTRONIC DOPPELGÄNGER'

The Mystery of the Double in the Age of the Internet

[24] You will have noticed something was said in yesterday's public lecture[25] that is of great significance for the acquisition of spiritual knowledge within human life. I spoke of those of our contemporaries here on the physical plane who prefer to acquire ideas that derive only from the sense world, or which are gained through an intellect that is bound to the sense world. I indicated how, after death, human beings who do not wish to know of anything other than the sense world remain tied in a way to surroundings that still fall strongly within the earthly, physical region in which the human being resides between birth and death. As a consequence, destructive forces are created within the physical world through such human beings who, owing to their life in the physical body, remain tied to the earthly, physical world for a long time after death.

In discussing such a matter, one touches on deep, profound secrets of human life, mysteries which for centuries, millennia one could say, have been carefully guarded by certain occult societies. These societies claimed (we will not examine today with what justification) that human beings were not mature enough to receive such truths, such secrets, which, if they were to become known, would cause great confusion. We will have less to say today about the justification for withholding from human beings such deeply penetrating truths, so significant for life, and cultivating them only within the narrow circles of occult schools. It must be said, however, that the time has come when wider circles of humanity cannot and must not remain without communications of these secrets about the supersensible world, such as I mentioned yesterday. Indeed, public communication of these matters must be taken further and further.

For even if it was appropriate, within certain limits, to withhold such secrets in earlier times when humanity lived under different conditions, that would no longer be justified now. As you know, we are in the fifth post-Atlantean epoch and human beings are now subject to other life conditions, under which they will necessarily pass through the portal of death as forces of destruction if they do not increasingly search in this life for inner pictures, concepts and ideas concerning supersensible matters. We cannot maintain, therefore, that those people are justified who say: well, we can just wait and see what will happen after death. No, between birth and death, one needs to know about certain things concerning the spiritual world of the sort that were indicated yesterday, in order to pass through the portal of death with these conceptions.

In earlier periods of humanity's evolution, the situation was different. As you know, until well into the sixteenth century, before the emergence of the Copernican world-view, human beings held entirely other beliefs about the structure of the world. It was necessary, of course, for human progress and for the advance of human freedom within humanity's evolution that the Copernican world-view made its appearance, just as spiritual science must make its appearance now. But with the physical world-view that human beings held before Copernicanism (today one can call it incorrect, if one so wishes)—the view of the physical structure of the world according to which the Earth stands still and the Sun moves around the Earth's heavens, the stars move around the Earth, and beyond the starry heavens there exists a spiritual sphere inhabited by spiritual beings—with this world-view, human beings were still able to go through the portal of death without being held back in the earthly sphere as the deceased. This world-view did not yet cause human beings to become forces of destruction in the earthly sphere after passing through the portal of death. That only came about with the sudden emergence of Copernicanism, the idea of the whole world spread out in space and only subject to the laws of space. Only with Copernican views that allow for the Earth to circle the Sun are human beings bound to physical, sensory existence and prevented from rising up to the spiritual world in the appropriate manner after death.

Today one needs to become familiar with this other side of the Copernican world-view, now that for centuries human souls have been conditioned through having the magnificent progress of the Copernican world-view placed before them again and again. The one side is as justified as the other. Today the one is deemed a sign of intelligence (though it is in fact a rather narrow-minded intelligence that holds up the Copernican world-view as the one true teaching). Whereas the other—that, due to their Copernican world-view, human beings remain bound to the Earth after death unless they acquire a spiritual conception, such as can be acquired within spiritual science today—is still considered foolishness and folly by people at present. Yet it is true, nevertheless. As you know from the Bible, many a thing that is foolishness to human beings is wisdom for the gods.

When human beings pass through the portal of death, they thereby alter the nature of their consciousness. It would be a completely false idea to believe that human beings lose consciousness after death. This peculiar idea is even prevalent among groups that call themselves 'theosophical'. It is a nonsense. For, on the contrary, consciousness becomes much more powerful, much more intense, but it is then of a different nature. Conscious ideas after death must be considered something else entirely, even when contrasted with our normal conceptions of the physical world.

After death, the human being comes into contact with those people first and foremost with whom he is karmically linked during his life. In the spiritual world between death and a new birth, the deceased may encounter many human souls, whom he penetrates—for the principle of penetrability rather than impenetrability applies there—while those whom he passes by, if I can use that expression, are not present there for him. Those who are present there for him are those with whom he has a karmic connection. Through our life on Earth we need to grow into a general relationship between worlds, even after death. The founding of societies established on purely spiritual grounds has already become a task for humanity of the present and of the future. Why does one seek to establish societies such as the Anthroposophical Society? Why does one seek to unite people in a sense under such ideas? Because a karmic bond is thereby established between human beings who are meant to find each other in the spiritual world. They are meant to be together in the spiritual world, which is something they could not do if they wandered around cut off from one another here. By creating the opportunity for human beings to share and spread spiritual knowledge and wisdom, we achieve an enormous amount for life in the spiritual world. This then acts back on the physical, sense world, which is constantly under the influence of the spiritual world. What occurs here are only the effects, the causes of which arise over there in the spiritual world—including while we live here on the physical plane. And you could say that, if we merely consider what today are often run purely for propaganda purposes, associations are founded for everything possible, but truly very few are dedicated to spiritual matters, even if they are founded out of ever such great enthusiasm. Through many an association, people think they are able to gradually transform the world into an earthly paradise. Well, prior to these three years of war, there were numerous such associations founded on Earth in which people worked towards gradually turning Europe into a social paradise! What exists now does not lend much credence to the belief that events will take their course according to how one thinks one is able to direct them.

On the other hand, however, collaboration of the physical world with the spiritual world is even more complicated. Nevertheless, it must be said that, if associations are founded in the light of spiritual science, people are working not only with the world of effects but also with the world of causes, which lies behind the sensory effects. One needs to permeate oneself with this feeling if one wishes to understand correctly the infinitely deep significance of what is being achieved at present through living together in spiritual collaboration and what will be achieved in this respect in the future of humanity.

This is not something that can arise out of any mere clubby association but a sacred task, which was destined for humanity of the present and of the future by the heavenly spiritual beings who guide the world. For human beings will have to acquire certain ideas about the supersensible world, as ever fewer supersensible ideas will come from the sense world. You could say that supersensible ideas are increasingly being driven out due to the continued progress of natural science. Human beings would therefore gradually exclude themselves entirely from the spiritual world if they did not acquire any supersensible, spiritual concepts. They would condemn themselves after death to uniting entirely with what is merely the physical Earth, and also to uniting themselves with what the physical Earth is destined to become.

But the physical Earth will become a corpse in future and human beings as souls would be faced with the terrible prospect of condemning themselves to inhabiting a future corpse, unless they decide to familiarize themselves with the spiritual world and put down roots in the spiritual world. The pursuit of spiritual science has therefore been set as a serious and profound task. That is something we must call before our souls as a sacred thought once every day as it were, so that we never lose our zeal for the justified endeavour of spiritual science.

If we take part in everything that comes towards us as concepts, all the many concepts that have already entered our spiritual stream from the spiritual world, then these conceptions can be expanded further and further. They enable us to free ourselves from our bondage to the earthly realm and to what is destructive in the earthly realm, so that we can act from out of other perspectives. We still remain united with the souls that we have left behind on Earth and with whom we are karmically connected, as well as with the Earth itself, but we are united with them from out of other regions. Indeed, we are even more intensively connected with the souls we have left behind on Earth if we are united with them in a sense from out of higher regions—provided, that is, we are not condemned through having lived a purely materialistic life to haunt the Earth, so to speak, where we cannot remain united through love with anything on Earth but instead can only really act as centres of destruction.

You see, here we gradually develop our consciousness from childhood onwards—well, we know how this consciousness grows and matures and need not say anything more. After death, entirely other processes prevail under which we must gradually acquire the consciousness that is required for life between death and a new birth. The way we go about our lives on Earth, having experiences and learning things, that is not how it is after death; it is then no longer really necessary. What is necessary is that we detach ourselves from the extreme intensity of attachment that remains with us when we have departed our physical body. By passing through the portal of death and into a relationship with the spiritual world, we grow together with the same spiritual world that we describe here through spiritual science. We describe it as the world of the higher hierarchies—Angeloi, Archangeloi, Archai, Exusiai, Dynamis, Kyriotetes and so on—as the world of the higher hierarchies and as the deeds and experiences of these hierarchies. Here the world is outside of us; we are surrounded by the mineral realm, the plant realm and the animal realm. When we have passed through the portal of death, the spiritual beings that we count among the higher hierarchies are there in us, indeed, their worlds are there in us. We are united with them; it is just that, initially, we are not able to distinguish ourselves from them. We live within them in that they permeate us. Admittedly, this is a difficult concept, but it is one that needs to be grasped: here we are outside of the world, there we are inside the world. Our being spreads itself over the whole world, yet we are unable to separate out and recognize ourselves. After death we are filled completely, so to speak, with the being of the higher hierarchies and with what these hierarchies do. What is required is that we first separate out the next hierarchies that permeate us, the hierarchies of the Angeloi, Archangeloi and Archai, from the higher hierarchies. Over there, we do not attain a proper 'I' consciousness at all (I have already described the gradual maturing of the 'I' consciousness in other lecture cycles and talks) if we are unable to find the power within us to distinguish. What in us is Angelos? What in us is Elohim? What in us is a being from the hierarchy of the Angeloi? What in us is a being from the hierarchy of the Exusiai, the Spirits of Form? Over there, we need to learn to distinguish; we need to have the power to detach ourselves from that with which we are united and from what it is that we wish to identify. Otherwise, it is in us and not external to us. Here we must come together with what is outside of us and observe it, while over there we need to detach ourselves in order that we can be united with it.

Given the way the world is at the current stage of humanity's evolution, we can only detach ourselves from what is otherwise asleep in us by acquiring spiritual concepts, these spiritual concepts that are so uncomfortable for human beings here because they have to exert themselves a little, exert themselves more than is the case with ordinary concepts. If we acquire spiritual concepts, then, after death, they develop into an enormous force through which we are able to recognize the spiritual world and comprehend it. This is very important. Today human beings find the acquisition of spiritual concepts uncomfortable. They prefer to go to presentations where they are shown all kinds of photographs and whatever else exists of that sort, so that, as far as possible, they need not think beyond the sense realm; they only have to look at everything. Or, at any rate, they only like to go to lectures where they are told about things that they have in front of their eyes all the time anyway. Human beings today avoid expending the effort required to lift oneself up to such concepts, which are more difficult to grasp here because they do not have an external object; their objects are the facts they refer to in the supersensible world. But over there, these concepts are the powers that show us the world as it is in reality.

Thus we acquire the wisdom that we need through spiritual ideas and concepts in order to have a light over there; otherwise everything remains dark. What is acquired as wisdom here is light over there, spiritual light. Wisdom is spiritual light. Indeed, over there we need wisdom in order for it not to be dark. If we do not acquire any spiritual concepts, then that is simply the best means for ensuring that we do not have any light over there. And, without light, we move away from the sphere that we should be illuminating, to arrive back on Earth, where we wander around as the dead, as centres of destruction on Earth. At most, one can then only be used now and again by a black magician in order to provide inspiration for very special deeds and destructive works on Earth.

Wisdom is therefore required so that one has light after death. But after death we need something else as well. In addition to the ability to separate ourselves from and distinguish the beings of the spiritual world, after death we also need the capacity for love. Otherwise, we would not be able to develop the correct kind of relationships with the beings whom we are able to see through wisdom. We need love. But love that is developed here on Earth is largely dependent on the physical body. It is a feeling, which here in the physical world is dependent on the rhythm of breathing. We cannot take this love over with us into the spiritual world. At the present time, in particular, it would be a complete illusion to believe that we could take the love that we develop here over into the spiritual world. We do, however, take over into the spiritual world all the power of the love that we acquire here in the physical world through our sense-bound perspective, through life with our physical being. Love is kindled by what is developed here in the physical world as understanding and appreciation for this physical world. The experiences that develop into love over there are precisely the experiences gained through the world-view of modern natural science, provided one has these experiences as feelings. However, love is something that can be of a lower or higher nature, depending on the domain in which it unfolds. If you pass through the portal of death and remain a centre of destruction in the earthly realm, then you will also have developed much love (for the fact that you remain on Earth is precisely a consequence of your having united yourself with purely naturalistic concepts). However, you will use this love for works of destruction, which you will then come to love, and you will be condemned to observe yourself in your love of this destructive work.

Love becomes something noble, on the other hand, if human beings can rise up into the higher worlds and love what they have mastered through spiritual concepts. Let us not forget, love is something that is base if it acts within a lower sphere and something noble, lofty and spiritual if it acts within a higher or spiritual sphere. That is the essence of what matters. If we do not become conscious of this, then we will not understand things in the right way.

It is concepts such these, concerning the life of the human

being after death, that individuals need to acquire for themselves today. It is no longer enough for present-day humanity, and it certainly will not be enough for humanity in the near future, that preachers tell people they should believe in this or that, or that they should prepare themselves for eternal life, if they are never able to tell people what the world actually looks like that human beings enter after they have passed through the portal of death. In earlier times, it was still possible to do this because natural-scientific or naturalistic concepts did not yet exist and because human beings had not yet been infected by mere material interests, which have gradually taken hold of everything since the sixteenth century. In earlier times, it was possible to talk to people about the supersensible world in the way that religious faiths still wish to do today. Today that is no longer effective, as human beings frequently entrap themselves—unfortunately, it must be said, out of deep compassion for humanity—precisely because they wish to promote their own eternal bliss in an egotistical manner through the religious creeds. They thereby entrap themselves more than ever in the physical sense realm, in the naturalistic world, and block their own ascendance after they have gone through the portal of death. They then experience something else entirely, which makes it a necessity to stress quite strongly that spiritual science must be pursued by humanity now and in the future because, it must be noted, those people who are unable to furnish themselves with any conceptions of life after death through spiritual science find themselves in a deplorable situation. Spiritual science is equally something that one must seek to spread among other human beings out of heartfelt concern, for the situation is wretched if people resist (and in their lack of understanding continue to resist) the emergence of spiritual-scientific ideas.

We must, however, be absolutely clear: the spiritual world is present everywhere. Just think, the world in which the dead are with the dead, this supersensible world, the links the dead establish with the living whom they have left behind, the links the dead establish with the higher hierarchies—this is all part of the world that we are standing in now. Just as it is true that the air surrounds us, so it is true that that world always surrounds us. We are not separated from that world at all; we are only separated from the world we enter after death through conditions of consciousness. It must be emphasized strongly (as even within our circles, not all our friends are fully aware) that the dead find the living again completely. We only remain separated while the one is here within the physical body and the other is without a physical body. However, all the powers that bring us together with the dead—through our detaching ourselves from them—first need to be acquired. Otherwise, the dead live in us and we cannot become aware of them. We must also carry over into the right sphere the power of love, which develops under naturalistic conceptions here, otherwise this power will become an evil force for us over there. It is love that develops under naturalistic conceptions, in particular, that could otherwise become an evil force. A power, as such, is neither good nor bad; it can be the one or the other, depending on whether it is manifested in the one or other sphere.

Just as we are connected with this supersensible world that the dead inhabit, so the supersensible world also projects in another way into the physical, sense world. Indeed, the world is complicated and an understanding of it is something that needs to be acquired slowly and gradually. But one must have the will to acquire this understanding.

The spiritual world projects into our world. Everything is

permeated by the spiritual world. Everywhere within the sense world, there is also a supersensible aspect. Human beings need to be especially interested in the particular supersensible aspect that relates to their own sensory nature. Now, I ask you to consider the following very carefully, as it is an exceedingly important conception.

We human beings have body, soul and spirit as our constituent members, but that by no means completes our being. Our body, our soul and our spirit are in a sense what our consciousness is initially concerned with; but that is not everything that relates to our being. Not at all! What I am going to say now concerns certain secrets of human becoming, of human nature, which need to become known today and become ever more widely known in future.

When the human being enters earthly existence through birth, he has, in that he has a physical body, not only the possibility to give his own soul its existence but—I ask you to consider this well—the human being does not know everything about this physical body by any means. For there are all sorts of things going on in the physical body that the human knows nothing about! He only learns gradually, and in a rather deficient manner through anatomy and physiology, what goes on in this body. If we had to wait with feeding ourselves until we had understood the process of nutrition, we could not even claim that human beings would starve, for it is not even conceivable that one could know something about what the organs do in preparing nourishment for the organism. The human being thus arrives into this world with his organism in which he clothes himself without reaching down into this organism with his soul. There is, however, an opportunity, shortly before we are born (not long at all before we are born) for another spiritual being, in addition to our soul, to take ownership of our physical body, of the subconscious part of our body. It is just a fact that, shortly before we are born, we are permeated by another being, whom, in our current terminology, we would call an ahrimanic spiritual being. This being is as much within us as our own soul is within us. Such beings live their lives by using the human being in order to be present within the sphere in which they wish to be. They have an extraordinarily high level of intelligence and a very highly developed will, but nothing in the nature of a life of feeling [*Gemüt*], not what we would call a human life of feeling. And so it is indeed the case that we go through our lives with a soul and this doppelgänger, who is cleverer, far cleverer than we are. This being is highly intelligent, but possesses a Mephistophelean intelligence, an ahrimanic intelligence, as well as a very strong will, a will that is much closer to the forces of nature than our human will, which is tempered by our life of feeling.

In the nineteenth century, natural science discovered that the nervous system is permeated by electrical forces—and natural science was right about that. However, if science holds, or scientists believe, that our nerve forces, which belong to us and provide a basis for our life of thought, have anything to do with electrical currents passing through our nerves, then they are mistaken. For the electrical currents are the forces placed into our being by that other being whom I have just described and do not belong to our being at all; we do also carry electrical currents within us, but they are of a purely ahrimanic nature.

These beings of high intelligence, but of purely Mephistophelean intelligence, and who possess a will that is closer to nature than what can be said of the human will, decided at a certain point, out of their own volition, that they did not want to live in the world to which they had been assigned by the wisdom-filled gods of the upper hierarchy. They wanted to conquer the Earth, for which purpose they require bodies, as they do not have bodies of their own. They therefore use as much of the human body as they can, as the human soul is not able to fill the human body completely.

Because of the way the human body develops, these beings are thus able to enter into the human body in a certain way at a particular time before the human being is born, and then accompany us below the threshold of our consciousness. There is only one thing in human life that they absolutely cannot endure: they cannot endure death. They must, therefore, always leave the human body in which they establish themselves before it succumbs to death. Time and again, this is a very bitter disappointment for them, as what they seek to appropriate for themselves is precisely the ability to remain in human bodies after death. That would constitute a great accomplishment in the realm of these beings, an accomplishment that they have not achieved as yet.

If the Mystery of Golgotha had not occurred and if the Christ had not gone through the Mystery of Golgotha, it would long since have been the case on Earth that these beings would have seized the opportunity to remain within the human being at the time when the death of the human being is karmically predetermined. Then they would have secured a complete victory over human evolution on Earth and would have become the masters of human evolution on Earth.

It is of tremendously deep significance that we appreciate these connections between the Christ's passing through the Mystery of Golgotha and these beings who wish to conquer death in human nature but who, at present, are unable to endure that death. These beings must always be on their guard so that they avoid experiencing within the human body the hour of death predetermined by the human being, avoid maintaining his body after the hour of death and extending the life of his body beyond the hour of death.

What I am speaking about now has also long since been known to certain occult brotherhoods. They are very familiar with these things and have withheld them from humanity (again, we will not examine with what justification). Today the situation is such that it is impossible not to gradually equip human beings with the concepts they need once they have passed through the portal of death. Everything the human being experiences here, including what he experiences below the threshold of consciousness, he needs again after death. That is because he has to look back on this life, which needs to be completely comprehensible to him in retrospect; it is the most awful thing for him if he is unable to do this. One lacks an adequate grasp of things to understand this life in retrospect if one is unable to shed light on a being that plays such a large part in our life as this ahrimanic being—a being who seizes ownership of us before our birth and who is always there and will always prefigure us in our subconsciousness if we do not continuously shed light on this. For wisdom becomes light after death.

These beings are generally very important for human life, and knowledge of them must gradually be grasped by human beings, and will be grasped by human beings. Only knowledge of them must be grasped by people in the right way; it must not just be spread within humanity by occult brotherhoods who turn it into a question of power, intending thereby to increase their own power. Above all, it must not be kept secret any longer for the purpose of increasing the power of certain brotherhoods acting out of egotism. Humanity is striving for universal knowledge, and such knowledge must be allowed to spread. It can no longer be beneficial in future for occult brotherhoods to use such things in order to increase their own power. Knowledge of these beings must increasingly be grasped by human beings over the next few centuries. Human beings will have to become increasingly aware over the next few centuries that they bear within themselves such a doppelgänger, such an ahrimanic, Mephistophelean doppelgänger. Human beings need to know this. Today, people have already acquired quite a number of concepts, but these are in fact blind concepts, as people do not yet really know what to make of them. I am saying that people are developing concepts today that can only be given a sound basis if they are brought together with the facts that underlie them.

And here something is opening up that must really be further pursued in future if humanity is not to undergo an endlessly impeding and endlessly horrifying experience. This doppelgänger of whom I have spoken is nothing more or less than the originator of all physical illnesses that arise spontaneously from within us—and knowing him fully is organic medicine. Illnesses that arise spontaneously in the human being, not through external injuries but spontaneously from within, do not originate in the human soul but derive from this being. He is the originator of all illnesses that emerge spontaneously from within; he is the originator of all organic illnesses. And a brother of his, who is not ahrimanic but luciferic in nature, is the originator of all neurasthenic and neurotic illnesses, all illnesses that are in fact not illnesses but just, as they are described, nervous disorders, hysterical disorders and so on. Medical science must therefore become spiritual in two directions.[26] That this is required can be seen from the inroads made by approaches such as psychoanalysis and the like (I spoke about this in Zurich[27]), which, although they deal with spiritual entities, do so with inadequate means of knowledge. The upshot is that one is unable to make any sense of the phenomena that will increasingly intrude into human life. Of course, certain things must occur out of necessity and even that which is damaging in one respect must happen, because the human being must be exposed to what is harmful in order to overcome it and thereby gain strength.

In order to fully understand these matters I have just described—that this doppelgänger is the real cause of all illnesses which have an organic basis and which are not just functional—one needs to know a great deal more. One needs to know, for example, that our entire Earth is not a dead, finished product, as mineralogy and geology believe it to be today, but a living being. Mineralogy and geology know as much about the Earth as one would know about the human being if one were only familiar with the skeletal system. Imagine that you were never able to perceive human beings through any of your senses but instead you had X-ray images of them. If your knowledge of people more familiar to you thus only ever extended to their skeletal systems, then you would know as much about human beings as geologists, and science in general knows, about the Earth. Imagine you entered into this room and of all the esteemed ladies and gentlemen you find assembled here you saw nothing other than their bones, then you would have about as much awareness of all those present here as science has of the Earth today. The Earth, which is therefore only known as a skeletal system, is a living organism. As a living organism, it has an influence on the beings that wander around on it, namely on human beings themselves. And just as human beings are differentiated with respect to the distribution of their organs within their bodies, so the Earth is also differentiated with respect to what it develops out of itself and with which it influences the human beings who wander around on it. I am sure you are aware that, when you think, you do not exert a particular effort with your right index finger or your left big toe, but with your head. You know for certain that you do not think with you right big toe; you think with your head. Things are thus variously distributed within the living organism, which is differentiated. In the same way, our Earth is also differentiated. Our Earth is certainly not a being that radiates up the same thing to all its inhabitants. Instead, in different regions of the Earth, very different things radiate up. There are different types of forces, magnetic and electrical, but also forces that rise up to a much greater extent into the living realm out of the Earth and which influence human beings in the most varied of ways at different points on the Earth. These forces influence human beings in different ways depending on geographical formations.

This is a very important fact, as what initially constitutes the human being—body, soul and spirit—actually has little in the way of a direct relationship with these forces rising up from the Earth. But the doppelgänger whom I spoke about is in a direct relationship with these forces streaming up from out of the Earth. And indirectly, by way of the doppelgänger, who fosters a most intimate relationship with what streams up, human beings, as body, soul and spirit, are in a relationship with the Earth and with what the Earth radiates out at the various points. These ahrimanic Mephistophelean beings who take ownership of the human being a short time before he is born have their own very particular natural preferences. There are those beings who particularly like the eastern hemisphere, Europe, Asia and Africa, and who choose to use the bodies of human beings who are born there. Others choose bodies for themselves that are born in the western hemisphere, in America. What we human beings have as geography is but a faint reflection of what for these beings is a living principle of their own experiencing; it is how they choose their place of residence.

From this you can also see that it will be one of the most important tasks of the future to cultivate again what has been split apart: geographical medicine, medical geography. With Paracelsus, it was taken out of the old atavistic wisdom and split apart; since then, it has hardly been pursued due to people's materialistic views. It will have to find its place again; many things will only be understood again once people acquire knowledge of the relationship between the illness-inducing being within the human being and the Earth's geography, with all that merges together and all that radiates out of the Earth in its different regions. It is important therefore that human beings become acquainted with these matters, as their lives depend on it. After all, human beings are placed into earthly existence in a particular way through this doppelgänger who has his dwelling within them, within human beings themselves.

All of this only really became immensely significant in the fifth post-Atlantean period and will become especially important for humanity in the very near future. That is also why knowledge of spiritual science must be spread now. It is especially important now because the present time calls for human beings to come to terms and engage deliberately with these things in a conscious manner. Human beings must become strong in our epoch, so that they can order their existence with these beings.

The present epoch commenced in the fifteenth century when our current period began in 1413. The fourth post-Atlantean period, the Graeco-Roman period, began in 747 prior to the Mystery of Golgotha and lasted until 1413. Since that time, we have been living in the fifth post-Atlantean period, which is only gradually bringing its particular characteristics fully to the fore in our time, although these have been in preparation since the fifteenth century. In the fourth post-Atlantean period, it was primarily the intellectual or mind soul that developed; now it is the consciousness soul that is developing within the overall evolution of humanity. When human beings entered the present period, their particular weakness in the face of this doppelgänger had to be taken into consideration by the guiding spiritual beings. If human beings had taken into their consciousness much of all of what is related to this doppelgänger-being, then things would have gone badly for human beings, very badly. Even during the centuries leading up to the fourteenth century, human beings had to be protected in advance, so that they should take in as little as possible of anything that was reminiscent in any way of this doppelgänger. That is also how knowledge of this doppelgänger, which was certainly there in earlier times, was lost. Human beings had to be prevented from taking in anything, not just from acquiring theoretical knowledge of the doppelgänger, but also prevented, as far as possible, from coming into contact with anything that has to do with this doppelgänger.

To that end, a very special arrangement was required. You must try to understand what took place at that time. In the centuries leading up to the fourteenth century, human beings had to be protected from the doppelgänger; he had to fade from their consciousness and was only gradually allowed to re-emerge in the present, now that human beings are called upon to order their relationship with him. This really required quite a considerable arrangement, which could only be achieved in the following way. Gradually, since the ninth and tenth centuries, conditions in Europe were so arranged that the European people lost a certain connection they had had earlier, a connection that had still been important for the people of the seventh and sixth centuries AD. What took place was that, starting in the ninth century and then continuing particularly markedly from the twelfth century onwards, the entire shipping traffic over to America was stopped (as it was at the time, with the type of ships that people had then). This may sound strange to you! You will no doubt say that you never learnt about anything like this in history. Well, history is in many respects a *fable convenue*, a legend; in earlier centuries of European evolution, ships had always sailed from Norway, from Norway of that time, over to America. It was not called America, of course, as it had a different name then. People knew that America was the region where those particular magnetic forces rise up that bring the human being into a relationship with the doppelgänger.

The clearest relationships with the doppelgänger emerge from that area of the Earth that is covered by the American continent; and, in earlier centuries, people sailed over to America in Norwegian ships and studied illnesses over there. In a sense, Europeans studied the illnesses caused by the Earth's magnetism over in America. It is there that the mysterious origin of the older European medicine is to be found. In America, where people were more sensitive to the influence of the doppelgänger, one could observe the course of illnesses, which one could not do in Europe. Gradually, however, one had to let the connection with America fall into oblivion. This was essentially brought about by the Roman Catholic Church through its edicts. Only after the fifth post-Atlantean period had commenced was America discovered again in a physical, sense-perceptible way. But it was just a rediscovery, albeit a significant one, because the powers that were at work actually brought it about that nowhere in the documents is there anything much reported about the older relationships Europe had with America. And where it is reported, one does not recognize it as such; one does not know that what is being referred to is the relationship between Europe and America in earlier times. The visits were, however, largely just visits. That the Europeans themselves then became the American people (as one says today, where the expression 'a people' [*Volk*] is misleadingly confused with 'nation') was only possible after the physical discovery, the physical rediscovery of America. Earlier, visits were mainly made to study the very special role played by the doppelgänger in the distinct nature of the American Indian race.

For a period before the beginning of the fifth post-Atlantean age, Europe had to be protected from influences emanating from the western world. And that is the significant historical expedient, the important historical arrangement, which was cultivated by the wisdom-filled world powers. Europe had to be protected for a while from all these influences, and it could not have been protected if one had not closed the European world off in the centuries leading up to the fifteenth century, completely closed it off from the American world.

A lot of effort had to be exerted for a period in the centuries of preparation to instil something into the European people that took into account their more subtle sensitivity. One could say that the intellect, which was to take centre stage in the fifth post-Atlantean period, had to be carefully protected during its initial emergence. What had to be revealed to this intellect needed to be presented to it in an especially subtle way. Sometimes this subtlety was similar to the subtlety in education, where sound punishments are, of course, also meted out. But all of what I mean here obviously refers to greater historical impulses.

And so it came about that it was Irish monks who, under the influence of the pure Christian esoteric teaching that was developing in Ireland, acted in such a way that Rome saw it necessary to close Europe off from the western hemisphere. For this movement wanted to go forth from Ireland spreading Christianity throughout Europe in these centuries prior to the fifth post-Atlantean period without any interference from what was rising up from the subterranean realm of the Earth in the western hemisphere. Europe was to be kept in the dark about all the influences on the western half of the globe.

It seems appropriate at this point to speak about these circumstances, which relate to Columbanus and his pupil St Gall. They were important individualities in the great missionary quest that sought to Christianize Europe by surrounding it with spiritual walls, so to speak, and by not permitting any influence to enter from the direction that I indicated. Individualities like Columbanus and his pupil St Gall, who founded and gave this place here its name,[28] realized first and foremost that the tender shoots of Christianization could only be spread by surrounding Europe with a fence in spiritual terms. Indeed, behind the events of world history, there are deep, profound secrets. The history that is taught and learnt in schools, on the other hand, is frequently just a *fable convenue*. One of the most important facts required for an understanding of the modern period in Europe is what began in the centuries during which Christianity was spreading from Ireland and lasted up until the twelfth century: efforts were undertaken through papal edicts at this time that gradually proscribed and suspended all travel by ship between Europe and America, so that the connections with America were completely forgotten by Europe. This forgetting was necessary, so that during the initial period in which the fifth post-Atlantean age was to be prepared in Europe, developments could unfold in the right way. It was only after the materialistic age had begun that America was rediscovered again to the west in the way that history tells us today. America was discovered from the east under the influence of the greed for gold, under the influence of a purely materialistic culture, the culture human beings are faced with in the fifth post-Atlantean period and with which they are required to establish an appropriate relationship.

These are matters of real history, which, I believe, also help to clarify what really is the case. The Earth really is something that should be called a living being. As a result of geographical differentiation, different forces stream up in the various territories. For this reason, human beings should not be separated into territories, but should accept from one another what is good and great in each territory, and what can only be produced there in particular. That is why a spiritual-scientific world-view seeks to create something that can truly be accepted by all nations and regions. Human beings must make forward strides in sharing their spiritual goods. That is what matters.

Over and against this, however, individual territories are quick to produce the desire for power, more power and yet more power. The great danger that the evolution of modern humanity will progress in a one-sided way can only be evaluated on the basis of concrete, truly concrete circumstances if one knows that the Earth is an organism, if one knows that what actually occurs emanates from the various points on Earth. In eastern Europe there is, comparatively speaking, less of this inclination purely through what streams out of the Earth. The nature of Russianness, for example, is intimately related to the soil, but the Russian takes very special forces out of the ground, forces that do not come from the Earth. The secret of Russian geography lies therein that the Russians take up from the Earth what was first imparted as light to the Earth, which is then returned by the Earth. In other words, the Russians take up from the Earth what streams from the outer regions to the Earth. The Russians love their Earth, but they do so because it is a mirror for them of the heavens. Therefore, however territorially minded the Russians may be, they have in their territorial disposition something which (although still at a childlike stage today) is extraordinarily cosmopolitan, for as the Earth moves through space it comes into contact with all the possible parties surrounding it. Furthermore, if you take up into your soul not what streams from below to above, but what streams from above to below and back up again, then what you are taking in differs from what streams directly from the Earth into a certain relationship with human nature. What the Russians love about their Earth, what permeates them, gives them many weaknesses but also, above all, a certain ability to overcome the doppelgänger nature that I have just been speaking to you about. That is why they will be called upon to provide the most important impulses in the age in which this doppelgänger nature will have to be combated and overcome, in the sixth post-Atlantean cultural period.

There is, however, a certain portion of the Earth's surface where there is the greatest kinship with these forces. If an individual moves there, he enters into the domain of these forces. As soon as he leaves, that is then no longer the case. After all, these are geographical, not ethnographic or national, but purely geographical matters. There is a region where what streams up from below has the greatest influence on the doppelgänger, and where, because the doppelgänger enters into the greatest kinship with it, it is then imparted back to the Earth. This is the region of the Earth where most of the mountain ranges do not run from west to east in the crosswise direction, but from north to south, where the magnetic North Pole is closest (for that is also associated with these forces). That is the region where, first and foremost, a kinship develops with the Mephistophelean-ahrimanic nature as a result of outer conditions. And much will be brought about through this kinship in the onward progress of the Earth's evolution. Human beings today must not proceed blindly with the Earth's evolution; they need to be able to see through and comprehend these conditions. Europe will only be able to enter into a correct relationship with America when such conditions are understood and when one knows what geographically determined effects come from there. Otherwise, if Europe continues to remain blind to these things, this poor Europe will fare the same as Greece fared in relation to Rome. This must not be allowed to happen; the world must not be Americanized geographically. First, however, this needs to be understood. What occurs must not be taken with such a lack of seriousness as is often the case today. For you see, matters arise for deep reasons, and knowledge is necessary today, not just sympathies and antipathies, in order to obtain a view on the situation in which present-day humanity finds itself so tragically placed. These are things that we are able to discuss here in more detail; they can only be hinted at in public lectures. Yesterday, I pointed out how necessary it is for what we call spiritual science to push through into social and political concepts. For America strives to mechanize everything, drive everything into the area of pure naturalism, and gradually wipe Europe's culture from the surface of the Earth. It cannot do otherwise.

These are geographical concepts, of course, not concepts that pertain to a people. One only has to think of Emerson to know that nothing is intended here in terms of the characteristics of a people. Emerson, however, was a person whose education was European through and through. Obviously, we are talking about two opposite poles that are developing. Precisely under such influences as we have characterized today, people like Emerson develop by opposing the doppelgänger with their full humanity. On the other hand, people like Woodrow Wilson develop, who are merely an outer shell for the doppelgänger. Through them the doppelgänger acts particularly strongly and they are essentially just embodiments of the American geographical nature.

These things have nothing to do with any kind of sympathy or antipathy, or any kind of partisan prejudice; they only relate to insights into the deeper reasons for what human beings are living through. Very little will be achieved towards the salvation of humanity if human beings do not enlighten themselves about what is really at work within the issues.

Today it is necessary again to restore the links with many things that were severed at the turning point in history when the route to America was blocked. And, as a symbol, I would like to place before you what you are able to feel and experience here in many ways: human beings such as St Gall. They had to prepare the ground for their work by means of the fence they set up. One needs to understand such things.

Spiritual science alone will enable real historical understanding. But, as you can see, prejudice upon prejudice will naturally arise against it. For how could one think otherwise than that knowledge will also become partisan! That is one of the reasons (which are actually reasons of cowardice) why certain occult brotherhoods have held these things back. They held back for the simple reason that these insights are frequently uncomfortable for people who do not want to become universally human. This applies especially to those who have the inclination to unite themselves with what streams out geographically.

[[29]] If you think back to what I indicated to you in this context, you will realize that there are numerous ways of making use of the streams that come from the spiritual world in order to cause harm here on the physical Earth during the fifth post-Atlantean period. There are a whole host of opportunities for that, one of which I pointed out to you today. I also said that it was necessary to stress that such knowledge needs to be taken into the consciousness of a number of souls, as that is part of the fundamental character of our age. The second half of the nineteenth century, in particular, was a very important time. I often described, in this and other circles of our friends, how 1841 was a year of crisis and a decisive year. Of course, one does not come to that conclusion if one merely looks at the events here in the physical world, but only by considering those events in connection with what takes place in the spiritual world. The year 1841 was indeed the crisis year that heralded the materialistic age. At that time, a very specific battle was begun in the spiritual worlds, a battle waged by certain spirits of darkness, one could say, who belong to the hierarchy of the Angeloi. These spirits fought this battle in the spiritual world until the autumn of 1879. They sought to achieve certain objectives, a whole range of objectives, of which we will only mention one today. At the time, between 1841 and 1879, it was to be decided whether a certain amount of spiritual wisdom could be made to reach maturity up there in the spiritual world, so that, from the last third of the nineteenth century onwards, this could gradually trickle down onto Earth, i.e. into human souls, where it inspires spiritual knowledge of the kind that, today, we call the knowledge of spiritual science. Such knowledge has only been possible since the last third of the nineteenth century.

The aim of these Angeloi spirits between 1841 and 1879 was to prevent this knowledge from reaching maturity in the spiritual world, from where it was to trickle down. But these spirits lost the battle they had waged throughout those decades against the spirits of light. In fact, to a smaller extent, something took place in 1879 that has repeatedly taken place within the course of evolution, and which has always been expressed by a certain symbol: the victory of Michael, or St George, over the dragon. In 1879, the dragon was also overcome in a certain realm. The dragon, in this case, are those Angeloi beings who aspired to achieve, but were unable to achieve, what I have indicated. That is why they were cast out of the spiritual world into the realm of human beings in 1879. It was thus a fall of Angeloi beings out of the spiritual realm into the human realm, where they now wander among people. They are present here, in that they send their forces into the thoughts, feelings and will impulses of human beings by variously inciting this, that or the other. They were not able to prevent (therein lies their losing of the battle) the arrival of the time in which spiritual knowledge trickles down. This spiritual knowledge is now here and will continue to develop further and further, enabling human beings to acquire the ability to see into and comprehend the spiritual world.

But now these Angeloi beings have fallen to Earth, they seek to pervert the course of what trickles down. Here on Earth, they want to guide that knowledge in false directions, robbing it of its good power and leading it into bad channels. In short, what they were unable to achieve with the help of the spirits over there (because they were cast out in 1879) they wish to achieve over here with the help of human beings. They are intent on destroying the good plan for the world, which consists of spreading among human beings, at the appropriate time, knowledge of how to control the masses, knowledge of birth, illness and death, and of other matters. Through premature spiritual births, they intend to spread such knowledge before its time. As well as seeking to instigate other things, these spirits operate in the way I have just indicated.

The only thing that helps human beings to counteract the influence of these ahrimanic beings is awareness. I repeatedly pointed this out in the Mystery Dramas; just recall the end of the last play.[30] Against certain aims of Ahriman, the only thing of avail is to know that he is there. The fifth post-

Atlantean age must develop to the point where many people, in a sense, speak to the ahrimanic powers and beings in the way that Faust does: 'In thy nothing, I hope to find the All.' They must acquire the habit of mind to look where the materialistic view sees 'nothing', and there to see the spiritual world.

[[31]] Inner necessities compel me at the present time to speak to our friends again and again, in the most varied of places, about an event that took place in the last third of the nineteenth century, an event that penetrates deeply and profoundly into human evolution. It is an event known to all occult schools, although they are frequently unable to recount the course of this event correctly. Today, I would like to indicate again briefly what is at issue. It concerns a battle of spirits, which took place in the spiritual regions from 1841 onwards, between certain beings of the higher hierarchies and other more superior beings. The beings that rebelled between 1841 and 1879, and who fought a rebel war during that period, had previously been used in the service of the wise leadership of the world. Even beings that rebel at certain times and become evil beings, beings of darkness, are good and useful beings at certain other times. Here I am speaking of those beings who, until 1841, were used by higher spirits in the service of the wisdom-filled guidance of the world but whose aims from this time on differed from those of their superiors. These beings fought a significant battle in the spiritual world, one of the battles that take place frequently, but on different levels, one could say. It is a battle that is presented in the legends and symbolically as the battle of Michael with the dragon. The battle ended when certain spirits of darkness were cast out of the spiritual regions and into the earthly regions in the autumn of 1879. Since that time, they operate among human beings, entering into human will impulses, into human motives and into what human beings are capable of understanding; in short, they act within everything human. Thus, in order to understand earthly events, human beings must become aware that there are certain spirits of darkness who have been living among them since the autumn of 1879. One could say, and it would be entirely correct, that the casting out of these beings in 1879 made the heavens free of these beings, but the Earth full of them. Since that time, their place is no longer to be found in the heavens, but on Earth.

If I had to characterize what these spirits actually wanted to achieve with their rebellious struggle from 1841 to 1879, I would have to say that they wanted to arrive at a point where they would be able to prevent the necessary spiritual wisdom, which will be revealed to human beings from the twentieth century onwards, from entering human souls. They wanted to deny it entry into human souls, in order to keep it above [in the spiritual world]. It was only by removing the hindering spirits of darkness from the spiritual realm that the human sense for spiritual knowledge could be opened up as a faculty from the twentieth century onwards, thereby enabling the descent of the spiritual knowledge destined for human beings. Here, however, where these spirits of darkness now wander among human beings, they are again making it their task to confuse people. They are seeking to prevent human beings from developing the right attitude towards spiritual truths, by withholding from them the healing purpose, as it were, of spiritual truths.

This can only be counteracted through a clear recognition

and precise understanding of these matters. There are certain occult brotherhoods, however, who have made achieving the opposite their task; they want to keep the wisdom in their tight circles in order to use it as a means of furthering their own desire for power. And this is the battle that we are in the midst of now. On the one side, there is the necessity to guide humanity in the right way, so that human beings take up spiritual wisdom, while, on the other, there are closed occult brotherhoods of a bad sort, who do not want to let this wisdom spread among humanity. They want human beings to remain ignorant and stupid in relation to the spiritual world, so that those who are in the closed brotherhoods can carry out their machinations from there.

The events of the present are thick with such machinations, and it will be to the detriment of humanity if human beings are not able to see that such machinations hold sway. It will soon dawn on you what actually lies behind these things, when I call your attention to certain truths that today are mature truths, truths that must fall out of the spiritual world into the realm of human beings, like ripe plums from a tree, but are prevented from spreading universally because human beings are afraid of them and thus have biased inclinations, prejudices and preconceptions.

In this context, I would like to speak in as concrete a manner as possible. The fact that in 1879 a number of spirits of darkness were cast out and have hitherto dwelt in the human realm has important and significant consequences. Above all, this fact has had the consequence that, since that time, thinking, clear thinking, has acquired much greater significance for human beings than was previously the case. There was never a previous time in the evolution of humanity in which one was forced to say, considering the inner evolutionary necessities, that clear thinking is now as necessary for maintaining physical life as eating and drinking. For if people think without clarity in these times in which we live, and in which humanity will continue to live in the future, then they will not be able to see in the right light those mature truths that are meant to fall from the spiritual world. Above all, human beings will not be able to comprehend the enormous, deep significance for the whole of human evolution of the Mystery of Golgotha, the appearance of the Christ within the evolution of humanity. Many people speak of this Christ Jesus. The theology of today, however, actually tries to prevent one from speaking of the deeper purpose that the entire evolution of humanity on Earth acquired through the Mystery of Golgotha. Of course, what is to transpire through the Mystery of Golgotha has only slowly and gradually come to pass. And it is only in this century that it has come to the fore in a very intense manner.

In ancient times, there was still an old inheritance from the time when people had an atavistic inner life that was permeated by spirituality. It is only in our time that human beings, if they wish for it, must work to acquire spirituality for themselves. That is why certain specific phenomena have only made their appearance in our time, in fact only since 1879. Today, our outer vision has become so coarse that these phenomena are actually only clearly visible if one casts the view of one's soul into the realm that human beings enter into after passing through the portal of death. After passing through death, souls that were born before 1879 arrive in the spiritual world in a different way to the way in which all souls will arrive that were born after 1879. What is at issue here is a deeply incisive event.

This deeply incisive event will cause human beings in their

souls to become increasingly similar to their thoughts, to what they consider to be the knowledge they have acquired. For people today, this may seem a strange truth, but it is a truth nevertheless. The ability to see things in the right light, to perceive them with clear thoughts, with valid thoughts, with thoughts that are soaked in reality, that is what is important and essential.

For example, if we view Darwinism correctly, in the way I tried to present it in yesterday's public lecture,[32] then that is a good thing. However, if we consider Darwinism a basis for the only view of the world that is valid, if we believe that the only true view is that human beings descended from animals, and if we live with this thought within ourselves—I descended from the animals, I originate only from such forces that also create the animals—then this leads souls in the present to become similar to their own thought conceptions. This is important because, when these souls have thrown off their physical bodies, they fall into the misfortune of having to see themselves as being similar to their own conceptions of themselves! If people believe (here in the physical body) that only animal forces were active in their evolution, then they will fashion for themselves a consciousness for the time after death that will cause them to see themselves as animals. For now that the character of the fifth post-Atlantean age has become manifest, following the event of 1879, the thoughts that human beings create for themselves serve the purpose of transforming human souls into these thoughts. That is why I claim that one does not need to have a particular liking for anthroposophically oriented spiritual science in order to choose to hold such views; one just needs to feel compassion for one's fellow human beings, who need these thoughts. They need these thoughts because they are creative thoughts for the life of the soul, because human beings in future are destined to become what they consider themselves to be. This had to come about under the wisdom-filled guidance of the world's evolution, so that human beings can truly arrive at a full and free self-consciousness. On the one hand, the gods had to grant human beings the possibility of becoming their own creations. But in order for human beings to give themselves, as their own creations, a supersensible purpose, for them to find a purpose in what they make of themselves and give them eternal direction, Christ Jesus went through the Mystery of Golgotha. And if one understands him, understands him in spiritual-scientific terms, understands him in thought, then one finds the way to him—the way that leads from an animal nature to the divine.

This truth is especially apparent to those who are able to cast the view of their soul into the world that human beings enter after death. Human beings who were born before 1879 still take a certain remnant with them that protects them from becoming purely what they were able to conceive themselves to be here. And, for a long time into the future, it will remain possible to protect human beings (these things are only gradually unfolding) from becoming merely what they imagine themselves to be. However, it is only possible through suffering, only if, to state the paradox, they are able to suffer themselves, suffer the unsatisfactory nature of their idea of the human being. Harmony within oneself and, at the same time, an understanding that allows the human being to remain human after death, will only emerge if human beings become aware of their true relationship to the spiritual world here in the physical body. Today, those who shy away from acquiring any specific spiritual knowledge because of their materialistic views are, of course, nowhere near to accepting that in 1879 such a transformation came about. Nevertheless, it is necessary for this knowledge to be accepted. From this, you can see that there is something that is becoming important, and will become increasingly more important in future, and that is the spread of what exists in the way of spiritual knowledge here on Earth. That is why the spirits of darkness, in order to promote their affairs, lay such great store by causing confusion among human beings, so that human beings do not reach the point where they are able to form the right thoughts here on Earth, into which they will transform themselves after death. The human being must become what he thinks himself to be.

[[33]] Now, the question arises: What is it, in fact, that present-day researchers are completely unable to consider, and indeed do not wish to consider? They acknowledge that there is a soul realm outside the realm of consciousness; they seek for a soul realm outside the realm of consciousness, but are not able to lift themselves up to a recognition of spirit itself. Spirit can never be grasped in any way by the concept of the unconscious, since a spirit that is unconscious is like a human being without a head. I have previously pointed out to you that there are individuals who, as a result of certain conditions of hysteria, walk down the street and only see the bodies, but not the heads, of other people. Not being able to see anyone's head is a particular type of illness. Among today's researchers, there are those who believe that they apprehend the whole spirit. But by positing it to be unconscious, they show that they have fallen for the delusion of believing that there could be an unconscious spirit, a spirit without consciousness, when we cross the threshold of consciousness (whether in the right way, as we always describe it on the basis of spiritual-scientific research, or in an abnormal, pathological manner, as always pertains in cases that confront psychoanalysts).

When we cross the threshold of consciousness, we always enter into a spiritual realm. This is entirely irrespective of whether we enter the subconscious or the superconscious. We always enter into a spiritual realm, a realm in which, in a certain way, the spirit is conscious, develops some form of consciousness. Where there is spirit, there is also consciousness. We only have to seek out the conditions under which the consciousness in question exists. We need to acquire the ability, through spiritual science, to recognize the type of consciousness that a particular form of spirituality possesses. Eight days ago, we discussed the case of the lady who leaves a social gathering, runs in front of horses, and is prevented from throwing herself into the river. She is then carried back to the house that she left, and is brought together with the host there, because, in some kind of unclear and unconscious way, she was in love with him. In this case, it cannot be said that the spirit, which was not part of this lady's consciousness, but which drove and led her, is an unconscious spirit, or that it is an unconscious soul element. It is something highly conscious. The consciousness of this demonic spirit that returns the lady to the one she loves illegitimately is, in fact, a much more intelligent consciousness than the one in the lady's own upper storey—by which I mean her consciousness. These spirits who stir and become active when the human being in any way crosses the threshold of his consciousness are not unconscious spirits; they are spirits who can very easily stir and become active on their own account. The phrase 'unconscious spirit', as used by psychoanalysts, does not mean anything. For, if I were to know nothing about it, I might just as well say, merely speaking from my own point of view, that the entire illustrious gathering seated here is my unconscious. It makes just as little sense to call the spiritual beings who surround us, and who take hold of the individual in cases such as the one I described to you eight days ago, unconscious spirits. They are in the subconscious; they are not captured by our consciousness that lives within us at the present moment, but they are fully conscious to themselves.

It is extraordinarily important to know this—especially for the task of spiritual science in our time—not because knowledge of the spiritual realm on the other side of the threshold, knowledge of real, self-conscious individualities, is an accomplishment of today's spiritual science, but because it is in fact an age-old knowledge. In earlier times, it was known in the sense of ancient atavistic clairvoyance. Today, it is known via other means; one gets to know it gradually. But knowledge of the real spirits located outside of human consciousness, who live under different conditions to ours, but who are continuously in relationships with us, and who can take hold of the human being in his thinking, feeling and willing—this knowledge was always there. And this knowledge was always viewed as the secret lore of certain brotherhoods, who treated it in their circles as strictly esoteric knowledge. Why did they treat it as strictly esoteric? A discussion of this question would lead a little too far at the present moment. It should be said, however, that particular brotherhoods were honestly convinced that the majority of human beings lacked the maturity for this knowledge. And, to a large extent, that was also the case. Many other brotherhoods, who are called the Brotherhoods of the Left,[34] also endeavoured to keep this knowledge for themselves. But they did so for the reason that knowledge of this kind, if it is taken into possession by a small group, confers power over others who do not possess it. And there have always been efforts to ensure certain groups have power over others. It was possible to bring this about by deeming a certain area of knowledge an esoteric possession, but then exploiting it to exert power over something else.

At the present time, it is particularly necessary for people to truly enlighten themselves about these things. As you know, since 1879 (I discussed this in the most recent lectures[35]), humanity has been living in a very special spiritual situation. Since 1879, especially powerful spirits of darkness have been displaced out of the spiritual world into the realm of human beings. Those who wrongfully keep the secrets associated with this fact within small groups are thereby able to instigate all sorts of things. Today, I am first going to explain to you how certain secrets that concern the present stage of evolution can be exploited in an improper manner. You will then just have to tie together closely what I will say today, which will be more of a historical nature, with what I will have to say about this subject tomorrow.

You are all aware that, for some time now, attention has been called within our anthroposophical, spiritual-scientific stream to the fact that the twentieth century, in particular, will bring human evolution into a special relationship with the Christ. During the course of the twentieth century (even within the first half, as you know), the event is to occur, as I indicated in the first of my Mystery Dramas, that the Christ will become a present reality within the etheric for a sufficiently large number of human beings.[36]

Now, we know that we are, in fact, living in the age of

materialism. We know that, since the middle of the nineteenth century, materialism has reached its pinnacle. But, in reality, opposites must coincide. The very pinnacle of materialism in the evolution of humanity must coincide, conversely, with the internalization of human evolution that will lead to the Christ actually being perceived within the etheric. It is understandable that the disclosure of this secret concerning the perception of the Christ, concerning the new relationship that the Christ will enter into with humanity, gives rise to irritation and reluctance among the members of certain brotherhoods. These are people who wish to exploit this event of the twentieth century, the appearance of the Christ in the etheric, for their own purposes, and who do not want to make it the common property of human knowledge. There are brotherhoods who are spreading the idea (brotherhoods always influence public opinion by spreading some example via means that are the least obvious to people) that the age of materialism will soon be over and, moreover, that, in a certain way, it has already passed. Poor, pitiable 'clever people' (here 'clever people' is in quotation marks, of course) spread the teaching, through so many books, gatherings and associations today, that materialism has run its course, that people already have some understanding of the spirit again. However, they are not able to offer anything more than the word 'spirit' and a few phrases. These people are more or less in the service of those who have an interest in stating what is not true, namely that materialism has run its course. For it is not true; quite the opposite, the materialistic way of thinking is deepening and will flourish best if people imagine that they are no longer materialists. The materialistic way of thinking is on the increase and will continue to become more prevalent for about another four to five centuries.

As I have often stressed here, what is necessary is that people must grasp this fact in clear consciousness, they must know that this is the case. Humanity will achieve salvation if one properly understands this fact, if one works within spiritual life in the knowledge that the purpose of the fifth post-Atlantean epoch is for materialistic qualities to be created within the context of the wider evolution of humanity. It must be countered, however, with all the more spiritual qualities. In the previous lectures, I explained what human beings need to experience in the fifth post-Atlantean period: the fully conscious struggle against the evil emerging within the evolution of humanity.[37] Just as, in the fourth post-Atlantean period, a struggle took place over people's understanding of birth and death, now a confrontation is taking place over people's understanding of evil. What matters now is for spiritual teaching to be grasped in full consciousness, not that we throw sand in the eyes of our contemporaries, as if the devil of materialism did not exist. His power will continue to grow and grow. Those who abuse these things know about the event of Christ's appearance just as well as I do, but they treat this event of Christ's appearance in a different way. In order to understand this, you must consider the following.

Given what humanity has become in this fifth post-Atlantean period, the following statement that many people make out of indolence is completely without justification: 'Well, while we live here between birth and death, what matters is that we give ourselves over to this life; after we have passed through death, we will discover whether we enter a spiritual world, we just have to wait and see. Here we enjoy our lives as if there is only a material world. After passing through death, well, it will soon be apparent whether a spiritual world exists!' This is about as intelligent as the oath made by someone who says: 'As truly as there is a god in heaven, I am an atheist!'[38] It is about as intelligent as that. But it is the way of thinking of very many who say: 'After death, we will see what it is like there; until then, there is no need to concern oneself with any kind of spiritual science.'

Throughout all periods of history, this way of thinking was highly questionable, but it is particularly fateful in this fifth post-Atlantean period in which we live, because it is made very appealing for people by the prevailing evil powers. In passing through the portal of death under the present conditions of evolution, human beings take with them the conditions for consciousness after death that they fashioned for themselves between birth and death. Human beings who, under the present conditions, concern themselves exclusively with inner pictures, concepts and perceptions of the materialistic sense world condemn themselves after death to inhabiting surroundings in which only the concepts they developed during their embodied life bear any reference. Those who acquire spiritual ideas enter the spiritual world in the right manner, whereas those who refuse to acquire spiritual concepts must remain in surroundings subject to earthly conditions, in a sense, until they have learnt to acquire over there (and this takes a long time) sufficiently many spiritual concepts with which they can be carried over into the spiritual world. In other words, our surroundings over there are determined by whether or not we acquire spiritual concepts over here. Many souls (one can only say this with pity) remain connected to the earthly sphere and continue to wander the Earth as the dead because they rejected, or were prevented from acquiring, spiritual concepts during their lifetimes here. And, in such a case, the soul of the human being, no longer separated from its surroundings by the body, no longer prevented by the body from acting in a destructive manner, the soul of such a human being becomes a centre of destruction if it dwells in the earthly sphere.

Let us consider then what, we could say, is the more normal case after death under the present conditions. Souls cross over to the spiritual world who did not wish to know anything at all in the way of spiritual concepts and feelings. These souls become centres of destruction because they are detained in the earthly sphere. Only souls who are already permeated with a certain connection to the spiritual world pass through the portal of death in the right way, so as to be taken up into the spiritual sphere and removed from the earthly sphere. They are then able to spin those connecting threads, including connections to those whom they left behind here, which are continuously being spun. For we must clearly understand that the spiritual threads between the dead souls and ourselves, who were connected to them, are not torn apart as a result of death. They remain and are, in fact, much more intimate connections after death than they were here. What I have said needs to be accepted as a serious and profound truth.

Again, the fact that this is the situation at present is not something which is known to me alone but to others also. There are, however, many who exploit this truth in a rather negative way. Today, there are misguided materialists who believe that the only life that exists is material life. But there are also initiates who are materialists, and who ensure that materialistic teachings are propagated via the brotherhoods. You must not think these initiates hold the absurd view that there is no spirit, or that human beings do not have a soul that can be independent of the body and can live without the body. You can confidently assume that those who are truly initiated into the spiritual world would never fall for the absurdity of only believing in matter. There are many, however, who have an interest in spreading materialism in a certain way, and who institute all sorts of arrangements to ensure that a large proportion of humanity believes exclusively in materialism and is subjected wholly to its influence. So there are brotherhoods headed by initiates who have this interest in nurturing and spreading materialism. These materialists are served very well if there is constant talk about materialism having been already overcome. This is because one can pursue a matter using words to the opposite effect; the methods for achieving this are often quite complicated.

What is it then that these initiates want? They actually know very well that the human soul is a purely spiritual being, a spiritual being wholly independent of bodily physicality, and yet still they nurture and foster the materialistic way of thinking in people. These initiates want there to be as many souls as possible who only acquire materialistic concepts here between birth and death. That way, these souls are primed to remain in the earthly sphere, where, in a sense, they are detained. Just think, brotherhoods are established that know this precisely, that know these conditions very well. These brotherhoods prime certain human souls in this way, so that the souls remain in the material realm after death. If these brotherhoods then make arrangements for these souls to come into the domain of their brotherhood after death (a feat that quite probably lies within their nefarious power), then the power of such a brotherhood will thereby be increased immensely. These materialists are therefore not materialists because they deny the existence of the spirit—they are not that foolish, these materialist initiates, for they know the truth about the spirit very well. They do, however, bring it about that souls remain within the material realm after death, so that the brotherhoods are then able to make use of them for their own purposes. In other words, these brotherhoods establish a clientele consisting of the souls of the dead who remain in the earthly realm. The souls of the dead have within them forces that can be directed in many different ways to achieve various effects. By these means, one is able to exert very special kinds of power over those who are not initiated into these things.

This then is just a machination of certain brotherhoods. You can only understand this matter clearly if you are not taken in by anything aimed at darkening or clouding your understanding, if you are not fooled into believing these brotherhoods either do not exist, or that their endeavours are harmless. They are not harmless at all—they are very harmful. Their intention is for human beings to continue treading further and further down the path of materialism. The aim of these initiates is for human beings to believe that, although there are spiritual forces, these are nothing other than certain forces of nature.

I would now like to describe the ideal to you that such brotherhoods hold dear. A little effort is required to understand this issue. Imagine a harmless world of human beings that has gone a little astray due to the prevailing materialistic concepts, which has strayed a little from the old, tried and tested religious conceptions. Think of such a harmless humanity. Perhaps we can imagine it better visually [drawing]. Think of this area here [larger circle, light] as representing such a harmless humanity. As I said, not only does this humanity not have a very clear understanding of the spiritual world, but, led astray by materialism, it also does not really know how to behave towards the spiritual world. In particular, it does not really know how to behave towards those who have gone through the portal of death.

Now, let us assume that here [small circle, green] is the area of such a brotherhood. This brotherhood spreads the teaching of materialism and ensures that these people think purely materialistically. In this way, this brotherhood manages to create souls for itself that remain in the earthly sphere after death. These souls become a spiritual clientele for the lodge [see drawing, orange]. In other words, one has created dead human beings for oneself who do not leave the earthly sphere but who remain with the Earth. By making the right arrangements, it is possible to keep these souls inside the lodges. In this way, lodges have been established that contain living as well as dead human beings, dead human beings who have become familiar with the earthly forces.

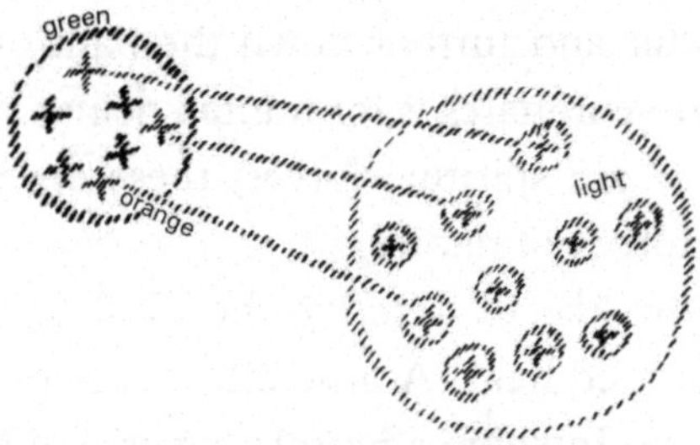

Fig. 2

Matters are then directed in such a way that these human beings take part in conferences here, or in spiritist seances, such as were held in the second half the nineteenth century, of which I have often spoken.[39] It can then happen (please take note of this) that what takes place is directed by the lodge with the help of the dead. However, it is the intention of the masters in these lodges that people should not know that they are dealing with the dead, but should believe that what they are interacting with are simply higher forces of nature. The aim is to convince people that these are higher forces of nature, pyschism, and such like, merely higher forces of nature. People are to be denied the real concept of the soul, and told that, just as there is electricity and magnetism, so there are also these higher forces. That these forces stem from souls, this is concealed, in particular, by those who are leading members of such lodges. As a consequence, however, those other innocuous souls become gradually entirely dependent, psychologically dependent, on the lodge, without being aware of what they have become dependent on, or from where they are actually being directed.

There are no other means that can be used against such things other than knowledge of them. If you are aware of them, you are protected. If you know about these things, in the sense of knowing them to be true, truly believing them to be the case, then you are already protected that way. But one cannot be too complacent about truly acquiring knowledge of these things (which can only gradually become clear, and I can only gradually bring the elements together in order to give you full clarity). For the moment, however, it is fair to say that it is still not entirely too late for this, since, as I have often called to your attention, many brotherhoods in the West introduced spiritism during the course of the second half of the nineteenth century on a trial basis, in order to determine, via this test, whether they had got humanity where they wanted it. It was a test to see how much progress they had made with humanity. In spiritist seances, people were meant to say that there are higher forces of nature—this is what the brotherhoods had expected. They were subsequently disappointed, these Brothers of the Left, that human beings mainly did not say that there existed higher forces of nature, but instead claimed that ghosts of the dead appear in the seances. This was a bitter disappointment for the initiates, as this was exactly what they did not want. The belief in the dead was precisely what these initiates wanted to take away from human beings. Thus, what was to be taken from humanity was not the influence of the dead, the efficacy of the forces of the dead, but the correct and profound thought that the effects stem from the dead. As you can see, what I have described is a higher form of materialism; it is a materialism that not only denies the spirit, but also tries to force the spirit into matter. You see, there are forms of materialism under which materialism itself can be denied. People can claim that materialism has disappeared, and that we are already talking about spirit. But they are all talking about spirit in a vague manner. It is entirely possible to be a materialist by turning all of nature into spirit, so that one ends up with psychism. What matters is the ability to see into the concrete spiritual world, into concrete spirituality.

Here you have the beginning of what will become ever more intensive in the next five centuries. The evil brotherhoods have now called a halt to what they had attempted. Nevertheless, they will resume and continue with these things unless a spanner is thrown into the works, which can only be done by overcoming one's complacency towards spiritual-scientific thinking.

In a sense, they have given themselves away through the spiritist seances. Instead of disguising their intentions by means of the spiritist seances, they have revealed them. In other words, this was more something that has shown up their calculated endeavours as having been not very successful. That is also why, from the 1890s onwards, there were efforts initiated by the brotherhoods themselves for spiritism as such to be discredited again for a period. In short, you can see how, in this way, by means of the spiritual world, deeply, deeply incisive interventions are made. What is at issue here is the pursuit of power through the exploitation of certain conditions that need to manifest in the course of humanity's evolution.

Work is being undertaken, however, to counter the materialization of human souls, to counter the banishment of human souls to the earthly sphere—after all, lodges are also in the earthly sphere, and if souls are to haunt the lodges and be put to work there, they need to be banished to the earthly realm. Working against this aim, against this impulse to utilize these souls in the earthly realm, is the profound impulse of the Mystery of Golgotha. And this impulse of the Mystery of Golgotha is also the process of healing the world by counteracting the materialization of the soul. The way taken by the Christ himself is completely outside the will and outside the intentions of human beings. In other words, no human being of whatever level of knowledge, not even an initiate, has any influence over what is being done by the Christ, which, in the course of the twentieth century, will lead to the appearance of what I have often spoken to you about, which you can also find intimated in the Mystery Dramas. This depends entirely on the Christ himself. The Christ will be present as an etheric being within the earthly sphere. For human beings, it is a question of how they are to relate to him. Again, nobody, not even a mighty initiate, can have any influence whatsoever on the appearance of the Christ. This will come to pass; please remember that. But one can make arrangements for this Christ event to be experienced in one way or another, so that the Christ event has this or that effect.

Indeed, those brotherhoods I have just spoken of, the brotherhoods who seek to banish the souls of human beings to the materialistic sphere, wish for the Christ to pass by unnoticed in the twentieth century. They want to prevent human beings from noticing his coming as an etheric individuality. And this aim is being pursued under the influence of a very particular idea, or rather a very specific will impulse. The brotherhoods are seeking to conquer the sphere of influence—which will be brought about by the Christ in the twentieth century and into the future—for another being. We will speak about this in more detail. There are western brotherhoods that are seeking to challenge the impulse of the Christ and to put in his place another individuality, who has never appeared in the flesh, an etheric individuality, but of a strictly ahrimanic nature.

All those arrangements I have just spoken to you about, with the dead and so on, they ultimately serve the purpose of distracting human beings from the Christ who went through the Mystery of Golgotha, and of passing over the rulership of the world to another individuality on the quiet. This is a very real battle, not just some abstract concept, or I know not what, but a very real battle that is being waged to instate another being in place of the Christ-being for the further course of humanity's evolution, for the remainder of the fifth, sixth and seventh post-Atlantean periods. One of the tasks of a healthy and honest spiritual development will be to extirpate and eliminate such efforts, which are most eminently antichristian. But only clear insight will be able to achieve something here, as the brotherhoods will call this other being, whom they want to make sovereign, they will call him

'Christ'—that is right, they will call this being 'Christ'! What will be crucial is that one really learns to distinguish between the true Christ (who will now also, in the manner in which he will appear, not be an embodied individuality in the flesh) and this other being, who will distinguish himself from the true Christ in that he was never incarnated during the Earth's evolution. This is a being who only extends into an etheric incarnation, and whom the brotherhoods intend to instate in place of Christ, who is to pass by unnoticed.

So here we have that part of the battle, where, on the one side, there is an attempt to disguise the Christ's appearance in the twentieth century. Yes, those who only observe life at a superficial level, especially in external discussions about the Christ and Jesus question, and so on, do not see into the depths. That is a fog, a haze, which is produced in order to mislead people by distracting them from the deeper issues, from the real concerns. When theologians have discussions about the Christ, there is always in such discussions a spiritual influence from somewhere, so that these people are in fact promoting entirely other aims and purposes from what they consciously believe themselves.

This is what is so dangerous about the concept of the unconscious; it is used today, even in relation to these matters, in order to lead people into an uncertain realm. While these evil brotherhoods pursue their aims in full consciousness, what they pursue consciously naturally becomes the unconscious of those who conduct all sorts of superficial discussions. One fails to grasp the essence of the matter if one speaks in terms of the unconscious, because the so-called unconscious is simply what is on the other side of the threshold of ordinary consciousness, a sphere in which those who do have knowledge of these things can implement their aims.

It is truly the case that there are a number of brotherhoods that are seeking to replace the influence of the Christ with the influence of another individuality, and who arrange everything in order to achieve this. But, you see, this is really one side of the matter, for, on the other side, there are eastern brotherhoods, Indian brotherhoods, who are no less interested in interfering with the evolution of humanity. However, these Indian brotherhoods pursue a different goal. They have never developed the esoteric means through which they could bring the dead into their realm, such as into the realm of their lodges. That is not in their nature, and they do not want such things. On the other hand, they also do not want the Mystery of Golgotha with its impulse to take hold of the evolution of humanity. They do not want that either. Yet neither do they want to challenge the Christ (who will enter into the evolution of humanity as an etheric individuality in the course of the twentieth century) by setting up another individuality, because they do not have the dead available to them in the way I described for the western brotherhoods. Instead, as they do not have the dead at their disposal, they seek to distract people from the Christ; for these eastern, Indian brotherhoods do not want Christianity to arise in strength. They do not want interest to arise in the real Christ, who went through the Mystery of Golgotha, who spent a single incarnation here on Earth for three years, and who is not able to have another earthly incarnation. They do not wish to use the dead in their lodges, but they do want to use something other than merely what they are themselves as living human beings. Instead of the dead, which are used in the western lodges, another type of being is used in these eastern, Indian lodges.

When the human being dies, he leaves behind his etheric

body; as you know, this is separated off very soon after death. Under normal conditions, this etheric body is taken up by the cosmos. I have explained to you in various ways how this process is complicated.[40] But prior to the Mystery of Golgotha, and, in eastern regions, also after the Mystery of Golgotha, there was a possibility for something very specific. When human beings cast off their etheric bodies after death certain beings can move into them. By means of the etheric bodies that were cast aside by human beings, these beings then become etheric beings. Thus, in eastern regions, it is possible to cause not dead people but all sorts of demonic beings to put on the etheric bodies that have been cast aside by human beings. And these demonic spirits, clothed in the etheric bodies of human beings, are admitted into the eastern lodges. Thus, whereas the western lodges have the dead themselves, who have been banished to the material realm, the eastern lodges of the left-hand path have demonic spirits, which do not belong to the evolution of the Earth but who sneak into this earthly evolution by putting on the etheric bodies cast aside by human beings.

Exoterically, this can be brought about by transforming it into a form of worship. You know that the calling forth of illusions belongs to the arts of certain brotherhoods. That is because human beings who do not even know to what extent illusion is present in reality can be very easily deceived by artificially produced illusions. What the eastern lodges seek to achieve is therefore done by clothing it in a form of worship. So, imagine I have a tribe of people, a tribe that shares a common ancestry. Having brought about the possibility in advance for the etheric body of an ancestor to be acquired by a demonic being, I, as an 'evil' brother, then tell this tribe that they must worship this ancestor. The ancestor is simply the one who has cast off his etheric body, which has been acquired by the demon through the machinations of the lodge. Ancestor worship is therefore introduced, but the ancestors that are worshipped are just some demonic beings in the etheric body of the ancestor in question.

The world-view of eastern human beings can thereby be diverted from the Mystery of Golgotha by working with the methods used in the eastern lodges. In this way, one achieves the same aim that, for eastern human beings, and perhaps for human beings in general (for that is the goal), the Christ as an individuality remains unnoticed as he passes over the Earth. In other words, the eastern lodges do not wish to substitute the Christ, but only wish for the appearance of the Christ Jesus to go unnoticed.

In a sense, therefore, a battle is being fought on two sides against the appearance of the Christ impulse in the etheric during the course of the twentieth century. These are the developments in which humanity is actually placed. Particular events that occur are really only a consequence of what takes place as the great impulses in humanity's evolution. That is why it is so sad that people are continually being deceived into thinking that the unconscious, the so-called unconscious, is active within them, in terms of the effects of, I don't know, repressed love interests or such like, when in fact the impulse of highly conscious spirituality is affecting humanity on all sides. The impulse remains relatively unconscious, however, if one does not trouble oneself to become aware of it.

In addition to these things, you also need to consider various other matters. Those human beings who have invariably been well-intentioned towards the evolution of humanity have always reckoned with what I have just described to you (there is not much else the human being can do or is permitted to do) and have undertaken on their part what was right.

A good place for cultivating spiritual life, an extraordinary good place for that, protected from all possible illusions, was the island of Ireland during the first Christian centuries. The Irish isle was properly protected from all possible illusions, more so than any other region on Earth. That is also the reason why so many Christian missionaries came from Ireland during the first Christian centuries. However, all these propagators of Christianity had to take into account a naive humanity among whom they worked. The European people among whom they worked at the time were naive, and their naivety had to be taken into account. Yet these people also needed to know about and understand the great impulse for humanity themselves. In the fourth and fifth centuries, Irish initiates, in particular, worked in central Europe. That is where they began and worked to prepare for what was to happen in the future. They stood, in a certain way, under the influence of the initiate knowledge that the fifth post-Atlantean period was to arrive in the fifteenth century (1413, as you know). This then was the influence under which they stood, which meant they knew that they had to prepare for an entirely new period; a naive people had to be protected for this new period. What was undertaken at that time in order to protect and fence off this naive people of Europe, and prevent certain damaging influences from entering?

Evolution was guided from a well-informed and, at the time, honest quarter, in such way that the shipping traffic that sailed from northern countries over to America was gradually suppressed. So that, whereas in earlier times, ships from Norway, in particular, sailed over to America for certain purposes (I will speak about these matters tomorrow[41]), it was gradually arranged that America was completely forgotten by the European population, and the links with America gradually disappeared. And, as we know, by the fifteenth century, the people of Europe knew nothing of America. The course of history was directed, especially from Rome, in such a way that, for specific reasons, the connection with America was lost, because the European people needed to be protected from American influences. A major role in this protecting of the European people from American influence was played by the monks from Ireland, who, as Irish initiates, were Christianizing the European continent.

In earlier times, very specific influences were brought over from America. But in the period when the fifth post-Atlantean epoch began, it needed to be the case that European people were not influenced by America, knew nothing about America, and lived in the belief that there was no America. It was only after the fifth post-Atlantean period had dawned that America was discovered again, as we know from history. In truth, however, as you may already know, the history that one learns in school is mostly a *fable convenue*. One such *fable convenue* is that America was discovered for the first time in 1492; it was in fact just rediscovered. The connection had only been cleverly concealed for a period, as this had been necessary. But now one needs to know again what the circumstances were and what really took place in history, which is that for a period Europe was very much fenced in and carefully protected from certain influences that were not meant to come to Europe.

These kinds of things show you how important it is not to think of the so-called unconscious as something that is unconscious, but as something that operates fully consciously behind the threshold of ordinary human consciousness. It is rather important that a larger section of humanity today is told about certain secrets. That is why I did as much as it is possible to do at present in public in the Zurich lectures. As you know, there I even went as far as explaining to people to what extent the historical life of humanity is not known to ordinary consciousness, but is in fact dreamt. I explained how the content of history is actually dreamt by human beings, and only when people realize that the content of history is being dreamt are they able to come to healthy inner pictures.[42]

These are the means through which one can gradually awaken consciousness. The outer appearances, the factual occurrences, they verify what I have said; only one must not overlook them. It is just that people pass by the facts blindly and asleep. They also pass by such tragic catastrophes as the present one, blindly and asleep. Today, I first want to impress upon your heart these more historical matters. Tomorrow, I will speak about these things in more detail.

I would just like to add one more thought picture to what I have said. Firstly, from what I have discussed, you will have seen what an enormous difference there is between East and West in the evolution of humanity. Secondly, I would like you to consider the following. Think of the psychoanalyst, who speaks about the subconscious, about the subconscious life of the soul, and so on. The use of such a vague concept to speak of these things is beside the point, as what matters is that one grasps what actually lies beyond the threshold of consciousness. What is it that exists there? There are certainly many things that lie below the threshold of consciousness. But what is down there is, in fact, itself very conscious. One needs to realize, however, what kind of conscious spirituality exists beyond the threshold of consciousness. Beyond the threshold of consciousness, one must speak of a conscious spirituality, not of an unconscious mind. Indeed, one needs to understand quite clearly that the human being has many faculties which he knows nothing about in his ordinary consciousness. Human beings would be in a bad situation if they knew, in their ordinary consciousness, everything that takes place within them. Imagine how they would have to arrange their eating and drinking if they first had to know precisely all the processes, physiological and biological, that take place in the ingestion of food, and so on. All this takes place in the unconscious. However, in all these processes, there are spiritual forces at work, even in this purely physiological activity. But human beings cannot first wait until they have learnt about what actually goes on within them before they can start eating and drinking, can they now? There are many things that take place like this within the human being. In fact, for human beings, by far the greater part of their being is unconscious, or rather subconscious.

Now, the peculiar thing is that this unconscious element, which we carry around with us, is taken possession of at all times by another being. In other words, we are not just this concatenation of body, soul and spirit. We do not carry our soul, which is independent of us, in our body through the world. Instead, shortly before birth, another being takes hold of the subconscious parts of the human being. This being is present in our subconscious; it accompanies the human being for the whole journey between birth and death. It enters into the human being just before birth and then accompanies him. One can describe this being, which occupies those elements of the human being that do not enter into the latter's ordinary consciousness, roughly as follows. It is a highly intelligent being, and one that, in its will, is similar to forces of nature. It is a being, therefore, that is highly intelligent and endowed with a will that is closely related to the forces of nature, a will that is much more closely related to the forces of nature than the will of the human being. There is one peculiar characteristic, however, that I must point out. That is, under the current conditions, this being would be subject to an extraordinarily grave danger if it were to experience death along with the human being. Under present conditions, this being cannot share in the experience of death. It therefore disappears shortly before the death of the human being in order to save itself. However, its aim is to arrange human life in such a way that it is able to conquer death for itself. It would be terrible for human evolution if this being who takes possession of the human being in this manner were also able to conquer death for itself, if it were able to die along with the human being, and thereby enter with the human being into the worlds that the human being enters after death. It always has to take leave of the human being before he enters the spiritual world after death. This can be quite difficult in many cases, and there are all sorts of complications that can arise. But the matter is like this: this being, who fully presides over our subconscious, is very much dependent on the Earth as a whole organism.

The Earth is by no means the kind of being that geologists, mineralogists or palaeontologists posit it to be, but a wholly living being. Human beings, however, only see its skeletal aspect, as the geologist, the mineralogist and the palaeontologist only consider the mineral realm, which is to say, the skeleton. If that is all you know, then you know about as much as if you entered here and, due to a special arrangement of your sight, you saw nothing of the entire distinguished company here than the bones, the skeletal systems. Just imagine, you came through the door here, and there were nothing but skeletons sitting on these chairs. I am not asking you to imagine that you consisted of nothing but bones—I would not ask that of you—but just to suppose that human beings only had the capacity to see bones, that they were fashioned with some kind of X-ray apparatus. That is all geology sees of the Earth; it only sees the bone structure. But this Earth is not only a structure made of bones, but a living organism. And, from its centre, this Earth sends out special forces to every point in every territory on its surface. Imagine the surface of the Earth like this [see drawing]; here the eastern region, here the western region—just to indicate the larger features. The forces that are sent up from the Earth are something that belongs to the Earth's life organism. And, depending on whether a human being lives in this place or in that place on the Earth, he comes into contact with different earthly forces. But it is not, or only indirectly, his soul, his undying soul, which comes into contact with these forces. The undying soul of the human being is relatively independent of the conditions on Earth (it can only be made dependent on earthly conditions by artificial means, as I explained today). However, indirectly, via this other being, who takes possession of the human being before birth and who has to leave him before death, through this other being these various forces act very strongly, influencing the human being according to racial types and geographical differences. It is therefore this doppelgänger, whom human beings carry within them, who is especially affected by geographical and other differences. This is extraordinarily significant.

We will see tomorrow how this doppelgänger is acted upon

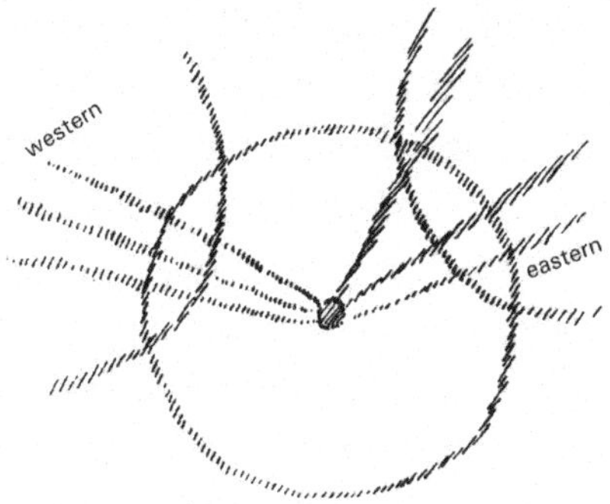

Fig. 3

at different points on the Earth, and what the consequences of that are. As I pointed out earlier, you will need to tie together what I am telling you today quite closely with what I will say tomorrow, as the one can hardly be understood without the other. We must try now to acquire the kind of concepts that pertain in a more significant way to the whole of reality, the reality in which the human soul lives with the entirety of its being. This reality undergoes various metamorphoses, but how it transforms itself depends greatly on human beings. One significant metamorphosis takes place simply through people becoming aware that, depending on whether they acquire materialistic or spiritual concepts between birth and death, human souls banish themselves to the Earth or arrive in the right spheres. For these things, the use of ever more precise concepts must prevail among us. In so doing, we will find the right relationship to the world as a whole, which we must do more and more. For that lies not merely within the purpose of an abstract spiritual movement, but, for us, it must lie within the purpose of an entirely concrete spiritual movement, which, in spiritual life, takes into account numerous individualities.

[43] First, I would like you to recall what I said last time I was here in reference to what we are considering now. I connected what we spoke about to the appearance of a new striving for knowledge through inadequate means, which led us on to broad historical perspectives. In relation to these things, and to what I said last time (for the same reason and out of the same impulse), I would first like you to note that what I am talking about are actual events, not just some theory, not just a conceptual system, but facts that I am communicating to you. This is precisely the point that we must take into account because, otherwise, it might be difficult for us to understand these things. What matters is not that I present historical laws or historical ideas to you, but actual facts concerning the aims and intentions of certain personalities who have banded together in brotherhoods. These matters of fact also relate to other beings, who have influence over the brotherhoods and whose influence is sought by the brotherhoods, but who, by the nature of their being, do not belong among human beings incarnated in the flesh, but are beings embodied in the spiritual world. It is most necessary that this is taken into account, especially in relation to matters such as I communicated to you yesterday.

In the case of these brotherhoods (you may have realized this from our discussions last year[44]), we are dealing, in a way, with various factions. I pointed out to you at the time that, within these brotherhoods, we are dealing with one faction that is of the view that certain higher truths should be kept absolutely secret. Alongside various other shades of opinion, there are, however, members of these brotherhoods who, particularly since the middle of the nineteenth century, favour revealing certain truths to humanity in a careful and proper way—even if, at first, only those truths for which there is a present need for disclosure. In addition to these main camps, there are factions with other nuances of opinion. From this you can see that what is intended, what is introduced into the evolution of humanity by such brotherhoods as an impulse, is quite likely to be the result of a compromise.

These brotherhoods, who are familiar with the spiritual impulses in the evolution of humanity, saw the arrival of the significant event of the start of the 1840s—the battle of certain spirits with more lofty spirits, which came to an end in 1879 with the defeat of certain spirits of an angel nature, spirits of darkness, in an event that is symbolized by Michael's overcoming the dragon. Thus, when these brotherhoods sensed the arrival of this event in the middle of the nineteenth century, at the start of the 1840s, they had to respond and asked themselves what needed to be done.

Members of these brotherhoods who, above all, wanted to take into consideration the demands of the age, were motivated to a certain degree by the best of intentions. It was they who acted on the mistaken impulse of wishing to take into account the prevailing materialism of the time. They sought to teach humanity, who only wished to know of things by physical means, something about the spiritual world in a materialistic way by these physical means. Spiritism was therefore launched into the world from this quarter in the 1840s on the basis of a good intention.

At the time of this battle, as I indicated, it was destined that, where possible, a spirit of critical enquiry, an intellect focused solely on the outer world, was to prevail on Earth. It was therefore necessary to give human beings at least a sense, a feeling, that there exists a spiritual world that surrounds them.

In the manner that compromises come about, so this

compromise also came about. The members of the brotherhoods who were firmly against revealing certain spiritual truths to humanity saw themselves overruled by the majority, as it were, and eventually had to agree to the matter. Originally, it had not been their intention to introduce these things that are connected with spiritism into the world. However, when it comes to body corporates and the will of body corporates, one is dealing with matters of compromise. And, naturally, as in public life, when something is decided by a body corporate, then not only do those who initiate the motion in pursuit of their own interests have expectations of what is subsequently agreed, but so do those who had originally been opposed to it and who will then also expect the one or other thing from it, after it has been decided.

In this way, well-meaning spiritual members of the brotherhoods were of the mistaken opinion that, by using mediums, they could convince people of the existence of a spiritual world that surrounds them. On the basis of this conviction, one would then be able to teach them further, higher truths. This would have worked if what had been assumed by these well-meaning members had taken place, if what had made its appearance through such mediums had been explained to people in terms of a spiritual world that completely surrounds them. What happened, however, was quite something else—as I indicated yesterday. What made its appearance through the mediums was interpreted by the people who participated in these events as having originated from the dead. Thus, what was brought to light by spiritism was actually a disappointment for all. Those who had let themselves be outvoted were extremely aggrieved, of course, that in the spiritist seances one could talk (sometimes rightly so) about manifestations of the spirits of the dead. The well-meaning, progressive initiates had not expected there to be talk about the dead at all, but had expected people to speak of a general world of elemental spirits; they were therefore also disappointed. But, above all, these things are followed closely by those who are initiated in a certain way. And so we have (besides the members of the brotherhoods already mentioned) initiate members of other brotherhoods, and, in some cases, of the same brotherhoods, in which minorities and sometimes majorities can form. We have to consider these other initiates, who are known within the brotherhoods as 'the Brothers of the Left', which is to say, those who exploit everything in the pursuit of power that, as an impulse, is incorporated into the evolution of humanity. And, naturally, these Brothers of the Left also had all sorts of expectations of what made its appearance through spiritism. Yesterday, I remarked that it was these Brothers of the Left, above all, who held seances with the souls of dead people. For them, what was of most interest was what would result from the spiritist seances. They gradually took control of the entire field, while the well-meaning initiates gradually lost all interest in spiritism, and even felt ashamed in a sense, since those who had not wanted spiritism from the start told them that one could have known from the outset that nothing would come of spiritism at the present time. This is how spiritism fell into what you could call the zone of power of the Brothers of the Left. Yesterday, I spoke of those Brothers of the Left who felt disappointed, above all, because they saw that what they themselves had initiated by allowing spiritism to enter the stage might reveal something they really did not want disclosed. For it might come out in spiritist seances, through messages from the dead, what certain Brothers of the Left did with souls of the dead, given that the participants at the spiritist seances believed they were being influenced by the dead. The very souls that were misused in a certain way by the Brothers of the Left might manifest themselves in the spiritist seances.

You must really take into consideration that what I am speaking of are not theories but facts that relate back to individualities. And if these individualities are united in brotherhoods, then, with regard to one and the same issue, one individuality will expect one thing while another will expect something else. When we speak about facts pertaining to the spiritual world, it is simply not possible to look for anything other than the enactment of the impulses of individualities. What one person does and what another person does can contradict one another in ordinary life too. If one is speaking in terms of theories, then the principle of contradiction cannot be violated. However, if one is speaking about facts, then (precisely because one is speaking about facts) it will often turn out to be the case that these facts are just as incongruous in the spiritual world as are the individual actions of human beings on the physical plane. Therefore, please always take that into account. After all, when speaking about these things, you cannot be speaking about realities if you are not speaking about individual facts. That is what is at issue here. Individual streams must therefore be peeled apart and considered separately.

This is connected with a very important matter, which, if one wishes to arrive at a reasonably satisfying world-view, one needs to have brought into one's consciousness first and foremost. What I am about to say concerns a profound matter of principle, even though it is somewhat abstract. But we need to have brought this fact before our souls.

Human beings who wish to create a world-view for

themselves are right to seek to make the individual components of that world-view fit together. They do this out of a certain habit, a habit which is as justified as anything can be, because it is bound up with everything that was humanity's most valuable possession of soul and spirit for many centuries: monotheism. We seek to explain what comes to meet us in the world as experience on the basis of a single universal foundation. There is good justification for doing this, but not for the reason that human beings usually believe, but for another reason, which we will speak about next time. Today, I only wish to bring the most important principle before your souls.

Those who approach the world with the presupposition that everything must be explainable without contradiction, as if it arises from a single universal foundation, will experience many disappointments when they face the world and their experience in an impartial manner. It is customary for human beings to treat everything they perceive according to a pastoral world-view, which holds that everything leads back to a single, divine source of being—everything originates from God, so everything must therefore be explainable in a unified manner.

But that is not how it is. It is not the case, because everything that surrounds us in the world as experience does not originate from a unified source, but from various spiritual individualities that differ from one another. Different individualities work together in order to create what surrounds us in the world as experience. That, at any rate, is how it appears initially. We will discuss other matters that lend justification to monotheism next time. But that is how it appears to begin with. As soon as we cross the threshold into the spiritual world, however, we have to think to a certain degree, indeed to a very high degree, in terms of individualities who are independent of one another. Consequently, one cannot demand that what appears should be explainable in terms of a unified principle.

Imagine this [see drawing] is a schematic representation of some human experience; the experiences, let us say, of 1913 to 1918. The experiences of human beings continue in both directions, of course. Naturally, historians will always be tempted to assume a unified principle for this historical development. But that is not how it is, for as soon as we cross the threshold into the spiritual world, which can be crossed from above or below, as it is one and the same [see drawing, red], various individualities who are relatively independent of each other [see drawing, arrows] are able to influence these events [of 1913 to 1918]. And if you do not take this into account, if you always assume that there is a unified foundation to the world, then you will never understand the events that take place in the world. Only when you consider the many various individualities working against each other, or with each other, all within the wash of the wave of events, so to speak, only then will you understand things correctly.

This matter is connected with the deepest of all secrets of human evolution. A veil has been drawn over this fact for

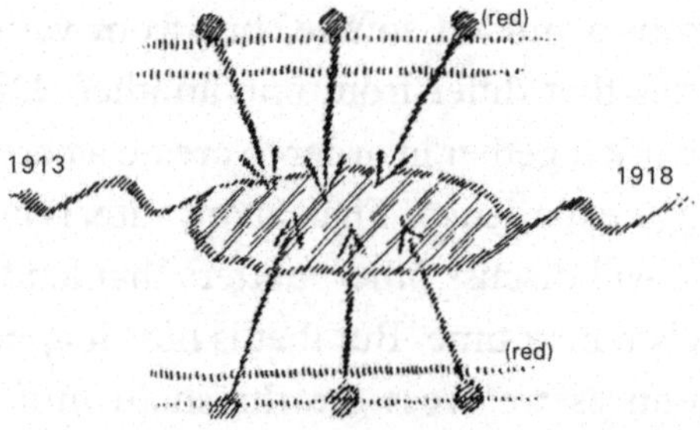

Fig. 4

centuries, millennia even, purely because of monotheistic sentiment; it does, however, need to be taken into account. If one wishes to make progress today on questions pertaining to one's world-view, then, above all, one must not confuse logic with the abstract lack of contradiction. An abstract lack of contradiction cannot be present in a world in which individualities work together who are independent of one another. That is why any striving for an abstract lack of contradiction will lead to an impoverishment of the concepts; the concepts will no longer be able to encompass the whole of reality. Concepts can only encompass the whole of reality if they are able to contain within themselves the contradictory nature of the world, which is the true nature of reality.

What presents itself to human beings as the realm of nature is created in a very peculiar manner. Different individualities are at work in nature too, in everything that we call 'nature', which includes natural science, on the one hand, and nature worship, the aesthetics of nature, and so on, on the other. In the current evolutionary cycle of humanity, a very beneficial arrangement has been put in place by the wisdom-filled guidance of the world. This arrangement enables human beings to comprehend nature with concepts that relate back to a unified guidance of the world, because what comes towards the human being from nature via sense perception as experience is only what is dependent on the unified guidance. Behind the tapestry of nature there is something else, which is influenced from a very different source. But this is switched off when human beings perceive nature. In this way, what human beings call nature becomes a unified system, but only because it has been filtered. When we perceive with our senses, nature is uniformly filtered for us. Everything that is contradictory within her is filtered out and nature is given to us in such a way that it appears as a unified system. But the moment we cross the threshold and draw on what belongs to reality in order to explain nature—the elemental spirits and the influences of human souls that can also be directed at nature—then we are no longer able to speak of nature as a unified system. Instead, we have to come to terms with the fact that we are dealing with the influences of individualities who combat one another, support one another, or strengthen one another.

In the elemental world, we find spirits of the Earth, gnome-like beings; spirits of the water, undine-like beings; spirits of the air, sylph-like beings; spirits of fire, salamander-like beings. They are all there, but they are not really of a sort that could form a unified regiment. That is not how it is. Instead, the different realms of the gnomes, undines, sylphs and salamanders are, in a way, independent; they do not merely operate as rank and file within a single system, but also combat one another. Their respective intentions have nothing to do with each other in advance. Instead, what arises does so out of the manifold interactions of the intentions. If you know the intentions, then you can see the combined influence of, say, the spirits of fire and the undines, in what appears before you. But you should never think that behind them there is a single entity commanding them in a certain way. That is not the case, although this way of thinking is widespread at present, especially among philosophers, such as Wilhelm Wundt (of whom Fritz Mauthner said, and not without justification, that he is 'an authority by grace of his publisher',[45] even though he was an authority for almost the entire world before the war). They assume that everything that lives in human souls—the life of thought, the life of feeling, the life of will—forms a single unity. They claim that, as the soul is a single unity, therefore all of these aspects must belong to a unity, to a shared system. But that is not so; significant discrepancies in the lives of human beings, which are identified by analytical psychology, would not be revealed if our life of thought did not lead us behind the threshold to an entirely different region, where the individualities that influence our life of thought differ from those that influence our life of feeling, who, in turn, differ from those who influence our life of will.

It is quite peculiar! Look, if this is the human being [see drawing, oval], and we have within the human being, the life of thought, the life of feeling and the life of will [three circles], then a systematician such as Wundt cannot imagine anything other than that this is all one system.

On the contrary, however, the life of thought leads into one world [W 1], the life of feeling into another world [W 2], and the life of will into yet another world [W 3]. That is precisely the function of human souls: to form a unity out of what, in the pre-human world, as it were, the momentarily pre-human world, is a trinity.

All of these things must be taken into account if we are to consider the historical evolution of humanity in terms of the impulses that get incorporated into it.

During the course of these lectures, I have said that each period of the post-Atlantean age has its particular task. In a

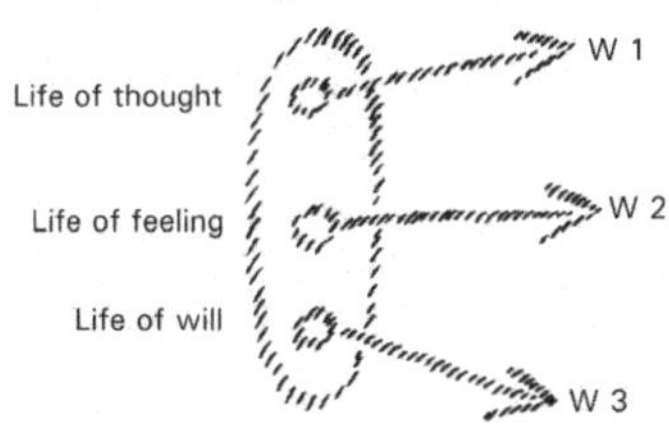

Fig. 5

general way, I described the task of the fifth post-Atlantean period by indicating that it is the task of humanity in this period to come to terms with the impulse of evil within world evolution. We have discussed what that means from different perspectives. There is no other option than that the forces, which if they appear in the wrong place appear as evil, are conquered for humanity. This must occur through the efforts of human beings in the fifth post-Atlantean period, so that they will be in a position to embark on something beneficial for the future of the whole of world evolution. As a consequence, the task of this fifth post-Atlantean period is an especially difficult one. Humanity, you see, will have to face a large number of temptations in future. And so, when the powers of evil gradually appear, human beings, under these circumstances, will naturally be far more disposed to giving themselves up to this evil in all areas rather than taking on the fight in order to place what appears to them as evil within the service of the good evolution of the world. And yet this must happen; evil must be placed in the service of the good evolution of the world to a certain degree. Without this, there can be no entry into the sixth post-Atlantean period, which will have an entirely different task, the task of enabling humanity to live, first and foremost, within spiritual impulses, in continuous perception of the spiritual world, even though it will remain connected to the Earth. This task of facing up to evil in the fifth post-Atlantean period is connected with a certain type of personal darkening that can befall human beings.

As we know, since 1879, the spirits of darkness, who are next closest to human beings, have been roaming the human realm because they were cast out of the spiritual world. These spirits, who belong to the realm of the Angeloi, are now present within human impulses through which they are able to exert their influence. I said that, in an invisible way, human beings are influenced by these beings, who are so close to them, and that human beings are prevented by the interference of the forces of evil from recognizing the spirit through their reason (for that is also connected with the task of the fifth post-Atlantean period). As a result, there will be many opportunities in this fifth post-Atlantean period for people to fall for dark falsehoods, and suchlike. In a sense, human beings have to make an effort to grasp spiritual matters through their reason in this fifth post-Atlantean period. The spirit will become manifest due to the fact that the spirits of darkness were vanquished in 1879 and, as a consequence, ever more spiritual wisdom can flow down from the spiritual worlds. Only if the spirits of darkness had remained above in the spiritual realms would there have been obstacles to this wisdom flowing down. They cannot prevent the flowing down of spiritual wisdom in future, but they can cause confusion from now on by darkening the souls of human beings. I have already described some of the opportunities that are seized to bring about that darkening. I cited the kind of measures that are taken in order to prevent human beings from receiving spiritual life.

All this does not give us any cause to lament, or anything similar, but a reason for strengthening the power and energy of the human soul's striving towards the spiritual. If human beings achieve in the fifth post-Atlantean period what can be achieved by incorporating the forces of evil in a positive sense, then something momentous will also have been accomplished at the same time. The fifth post-Atlantean period will then have acquired knowledge of something for the evolution of humanity out of a greater vision than in any other post-Atlantean period, than in any earlier period in the Earth's evolution. For example, the Christ appeared through the Mystery of Golgotha to the fourth post-Atlantean period, but to make him part of human reason can only be achieved in the fifth post-Atlantean period. In the fourth post-Atlantean period, human beings were able to grasp that, in the Christ impulse, they have something that leads them beyond death as souls; that was made sufficiently clear through Pauline Christianity. But something even more significant will occur for the evolution of the fifth post-Atlantean period, in that human souls will recognize that they have in Christ the helper they need to transform the forces of evil into good. There is one thing that is connected with this particular characteristic of the fifth post-Atlantean period, something that one should inscribe into one's soul every day anew. It is something that one should not forget, even though the human being is particularly disposed to forgetting this matter. That is, the human being in the fifth post-Atlantean period must be a fighter for the spirit; he will experience a dwindling of his forces if he does not continually control them in order to use them to conquer the spiritual world. In the fifth post-Atlantean period, the human being is left to his own freedom to the highest degree! This is something he must experience. And, in a way, everything that human beings encounter in this fifth post-Atlantean period must be measured against the idea of human freedom. For if the forces of human beings were to dwindle, then everything could turn out for the worse, so to speak. Human beings are not in a position, in this fifth post-Atlantean period, to be led like children. If there are certain brotherhoods that, in a way, hold up the ideal of leading human beings like children, as they were led in the third and fourth post-Atlantean periods, then these brotherhoods are not doing the right thing at all; they are not doing what actually needs to happen for the evolution of humanity. Anyone who speaks of the spiritual world in the fifth post-Atlantean period must always, time and again, point to the spiritual world in such a way that its acceptance or rejection is left entirely to the freedom of human beings. That is why, in the fifth post-Atlantean period, certain things can only be stated; but the stating of these things is now just as important as whatever else was important in other ages. I will give you an example of this.

In our time, the communication of truths, if I may speak trivially, the presentation of truths is the most important thing. Human beings should then align themselves according to these truths out of their own freedom. One should not actually go any further than the presentation, than the communication of truths; the rest should follow out of a free decision. It should follow in the way that things come about following decisions that have been reached out of the impulse of the physical plane. This also applies to matters that, to a certain extent, can only be led and guided by the spiritual world itself.

We will understand one another better straightaway if we examine this in detail. In the fourth post-Atlantean period, it was still the case that other things mattered more than just the mere word, the mere act of communication. What was it that mattered? Let us consider a particular case. The island we call Ireland today has some very special characteristics. This Irish isle differs from the whole of the rest of the Earth in certain respects. All regions of the Earth differ from one another in certain ways—that itself is therefore not something that is special. Today, however, I wish to emphasize the relatively strong difference that exists between Ireland and all the other areas of the Earth. It is possible to go back through the evolution of the Earth (as you know from my *Occult Science, an Outline*) and establish the various influences, the various events, from what can be brought out of the spiritual world as facts. From *Occult Science*, you know what the situation was like if you go back to what is called the Lemurian period—what has happened since the Lemurian period, how various things have since developed. Yesterday, I pointed out to you that the whole of the Earth should actually be considered an organism, and that in the various territories it radiates out different things to its inhabitants. What is emitted has a very special influence on the doppelgänger, as I pointed out yesterday towards the end [of the lecture]. In the case of Ireland, it is such that, in ancient times, the various people who lived there brought the peculiarity of Ireland to expression in fairy-tale form as a legend. People were familiar with an esoteric legend, which, you could say, was expressive of the being of Ireland within the Earth's organism. It was said that, once upon a time, human beings had been driven out of Paradise because, in Paradise, they had been seduced by Lucifer. It was then said that humanity had been scattered throughout the rest of the world, which already existed at the time when humanity was driven out. One therefore distinguished Paradise with Lucifer in it from the rest of the Earth into which humanity was cast out (that is how the legend presented it in fairy-tale form). This did not apply to Ireland, however, as it did not belong to the rest of the world in same sense, because, before Lucifer entered Paradise, a mirror image of Paradise was formed on Earth, and that mirror image was what became Ireland.

One therefore needs to understand that Ireland is the

region of the Earth which has no part in Lucifer, a region with which Lucifer has no relationship. What had to be separated from Paradise, so that an earthly reflection of Paradise could be created, would have prevented Lucifer from entering into Paradise. In other words, Ireland, according to this legend, was a part of Paradise that had been separated off because, otherwise, it would have prevented Lucifer from entering into Paradise. Only after Ireland had been separated from Paradise was Lucifer able to enter into Paradise.

What I have just presented to you rather imperfectly is a very beautiful, esoteric legend. For centuries, it was for many people the explanation of Ireland's very special task. In my first Mystery Drama, you will find a portrayal of what I have often told you about: the Christianization of Europe led by Irish monks.[46] When St Patrick introduced Christianity to Ireland, the situation was such that it led people to a religious piety of the highest order. The piety that prevailed in the Christian monasteries even resulted in a renaming of Ireland, which can be seen as a reinterpretation of the legend that I have just been speaking about. At the time when the best impulses of European Christendom sent forth Irish initiates, who had been lovingly initiated into Christianity, Ireland (which the Greeks had called 'Ierne' and the Romans had called 'Ivernia' [Hibernia]) was renamed the Island of the Saints.

This is connected with the territorial forces that I spoke about, which rise up out of the Earth and take hold of the doppelgänger. In the case of the Irish isle, these are the very best of those forces.

If that is so, you will say, then the best of all human beings must be found in Ireland. Well, that is not how the world is, of course. People migrate to other regions and have descendants, and so on. In other words, it is not the case that the human being is merely the result of a certain piece of the Earth on which he stands. It can certainly be the case that what rises up out of the Earth contradicts the character of the individual. You must not identify what truly develops within human beings with characteristics of the Earth's organism in relation to particular territories. To do so would be to enter the world of illusion again.

However, we can say certain things today, such as I have just pointed out to you now, namely that Ireland is very special ground. Statements of this kind might generate a factor, which, among many factors, could lead to fruitful socio-political ideas today. These kind of factors need to be taken into account as realities. What I have just said about Ireland is a factor; all factors of this kind should be taken into account and pieced together. That would constitute an applied science of human affairs on Earth. Until such a science exists, the arrangement of public affairs will not lead to any real salvation. What can be said out of knowledge of the spiritual world would need to flow into the arrangements that are instituted. For this reason, I have said in public lectures that it is important for everyone who deals with public affairs, statesmen and suchlike, to familiarize themselves with these things, as it is the only way they will be able to master reality. They do not do this, of course, and certainly have not done so hitherto. It is necessary, nevertheless.

What is important today in regard to the tasks of the fifth post-Atlantean period is the act of stating, the act of communicating. Before what is said can become deed, collective decisions must be reached in the way people reach decisions out of the impulse of the physical plane. It was different in earlier times, when it was still possible to act in other ways.

At a particular point in time during the third post-Atlantean period, a certain brotherhood arranged for a large number of settlers from Asia Minor to be sent to the island of Ireland. These colonists, who had originated from the same region of Asia where later the philosopher Thales came from, then settled in Ireland. You can read about the philosophy of Thales in my *Riddles of Philosophy*.[47] Thales hailed from the same region, albeit at a later time, as he was born in the fourth post-Atlantean period. But earlier, out of the same milieu, out of the very spiritual substance that later gave rise to the philosopher Thales, initiates sent settlers to Ireland. Why was that? Because they knew about the unique characteristic of the region of the Earth that is Ireland. They knew what was indicated by the esoteric legend that I told you about. They knew that the forces that rise out of the Earth though the ground of the Irish isle have little influence on the development of intellectuality, little influence on the development of egoism, and little influence on the development of resoluteness within human beings. The initiates who sent the settlers there knew this very well, and chose people who appeared suitable based on their particular karmic abilities to be exposed to the influences of the island of Ireland. There are still descendants today of that ancient population that was transplanted there from Asia Minor. That population was to advance in such a way that not even the smallest streak of intellectuality, nor the smallest streak of reason, nor the smallest streak of resoluteness should develop. Instead, however, there should be an extraordinary development of the life of feeling.

Preparations had thus been made well in advance for what later took place as the peaceful spread and glorious development of Christianity in Ireland, from where the

Christianization of Europe radiated out. This had been prepared well in advance. The fellow countrymen of the later Thales sent people there who subsequently proved themselves suited to becoming the kind of monks who were able to exert influence in the way that I indicated. Many such things were done in ancient times, and if you find the colonizations of the ancients described in the outer, exoteric history of today's ignorant historians (who may possess great intellects, of course, as intelligence can be picked up on the street today), then you always need to be aware that, in such colonizations, there was a profound wisdom. This wisdom led and guided these colonizations by always taking into consideration what was to take place in the future; in that, in those times, one took into account the peculiarities of the Earth's evolution.

That was a different way of planting spiritual wisdom into the world. Those who follow the right-hand path today could no longer do something like this; in order to divide up the Earth, they cannot simply order people to do things against their will. Instead, they have to reveal the truths, leaving people free to arrange their affairs accordingly.

Here you see an indication of the significant progress that was made from the third and fourth to the fifth post-Atlantean period. This kind of thing needs to be looked at very closely; one needs to recognize how the impulse of freedom must run through all that governs the fifth post-Atlantean period. Opposing this freedom in the human life of feeling is the adversary, who, as I told you, accompanies the human being from the time of birth up until death like a doppelgänger, but who has to leave the human being before death occurs. If one is under the influence of what acts directly through the doppelgänger, then all sorts of things will be revealed that can be revealed in this fifth post-Atlantean period. However, they are not suited to the task of the fifth post-Atlantean period because, in the battle with evil, they do not afford any opportunities for transforming evil into good to a certain degree.

Think about what actually lies behind all the circumstances into which the human being is placed in the fifth post-Atlantean period. The individual facts need to be illuminated in the right way; they need to be understood because, where the doppelgänger acts strongly, which I spoke about yesterday, there people are working against the true tendency of the fifth post-Atlantean period. Only humanity is not ready yet to evaluate the facts correctly in this fifth post-Atlantean period; especially after these last three tragic years [of war], humanity is not yet able to evaluate the facts correctly in any way whatsoever.

From what I have discussed today, take with you something that may, at first, appear to relate to an affair that is only very distantly connected to what I have been speaking about. The case that I want to present to you is this. At a large ironworks, tens of thousands of tonnes of cast iron were to be loaded onto railway trains. Naturally, a certain number of workers were employed for that purpose. Seventy-five men were to carry out the work and, it turned out, each man was able to load 12½ tonnes per day—thus, 12½ tonnes a day for each of the 75 men.

There was a man called Taylor, who was a man who gave more heed to the doppelgänger than to what must be conquered for the progress of humanity, for the human life of feeling in the fifth post-Atlantean period.[48] This man first asked the manufacturers whether they did not believe that a single man could, in fact, load much more than 12½ tonnes per day. The manufacturers said that a worker could manage to load at most 18 tonnes per day. Then Taylor replied: 'In that case, let us carry out some experiments; we would like to experiment with this.'

He then went about experimenting with the people. This is how the nature of the machine is transferred to human social life. There were to be experiments conducted with human beings! He tested whether it really was the case, as the practically minded manufacturers had said, that a man can load at most 18 tonnes per day. He instituted break times that he calculated on a physiological basis in such a way that the men were able to gather just as much strength in these breaks as the effort they had expended beforehand. It turned out, of course, that depending on circumstances the results were so-and-so much for the one man, and so-and-so much for another. Taylor then applied an arithmetic average—in a mechanism, as you know, you are free to use an arithmetic average, whereas in the case of human beings you cannot use an arithmetic average, as every individual is entitled to his existence—which is to say, Taylor selected those workers who, in total, took more efficient breaks, which he then allowed them to take. The others, who were not able to restore their strength within these break times, were simply thrown out. It then turned out that, after experimenting with the men in this way, those who had been selected based on their ability to recover fully in the breaks were each able to load 47½ tonnes.

The mechanism of Darwinian theory was thus applied to the lives of the workers; the unfit were cast away, the fittest were chosen by selection. The fittest were those who, with the proper use of the break times, were able to load, not the maximum of 18 tonnes that had been assumed before, but

47½ tonnes. In this way, it was also possible to please the workers, as huge savings were made, and one was able to increase the salaries of the workers that had been selected by 60 per cent. So, in addition, one was able to turn those who had been selected, the fittest in the fight for survival, into very satisfied people. But . . . the unfit were left to starve!

Here we have the beginnings of a principle. Little attention is paid to such things because they are not viewed in the light of overarching perspectives. But light must be shed on them from overarching perspectives. Today, we are still talking about a mere application of mistaken natural-scientific ideas to human life. The impulse remains, however, and will be applied to what will arrive in the course of the fifth post-Atlantean period as occult truths. Although Darwinism does not contain any occult truths, its application would lead to great abominations: the application of the Darwinian way of thinking through a direct experimentation with human beings. When occult truths truly arrive, which must be revealed during the course of the fifth post-Atlantean period, it would then be possible to gain tremendous power over people in this way, albeit only by always selecting the fittest. If one not only selected the fittest, but also sought to make the fittest ever more fit by means of a certain occult discovery, one would end up with a tremendous exploitation of power. This would work in the opposite direction to the propensity for the good in the fifth post-Atlantean period.

I only wanted to mention these matters in the way I have just described them to you, in order to show you how intentions that circumscribe the future have their beginnings, and how one must shed light on these things from certain overarching perspectives. It will be my aim next time to point out the three or four great truths to you that human beings in the fifth post-Atlantean period must arrive at. In doing so, I will show how these truths can be misused if they are not applied in accordance with the propensity for what is right and good in the fifth post-Atlantean period, but are used primarily to meet the demands of the doppelgänger, who is represented by those brotherhoods that wish to instate another being in place of the Christ.

[49] I would like to again bring it to your attention that humanity in this fifth post-Atlantean period will have to find a special approach to dealing with great life questions, which have been obscured in a certain way through the guiding wisdom of the past. I have already indicated what these great life questions are, one of which can be characterized by saying that there needs to be an effort to bring the spiritual-etheric into the service of outer practical life. I have called your attention to the fact that the fifth post-Atlantean period will have to solve the problem of how human states of mind, movements within the human soul, can be transferred in oscillating waves to machines, and how the human being must be brought into connection with what must become more and more mechanical.[50] I therefore pointed out here, eight days ago, the external way in which this mechanization is taking place. I described how it originates from a certain part of our Earth's surface, and I gave you an example of how, based on the American way of thinking, efforts are being made to extend the essence of what is machine-like to human life itself. I gave the example of work breaks that are to be used in such a way that, instead of a few tonnes, nearly 50 tonnes can be loaded by a group of workers. For this to be achieved, all

that is required is for the Darwinian principle of selection to be introduced into life.

In these places, the will is there to yoke the power of human beings to the power of machines. Matters such as this must not be treated as if they needed to be opposed. That would be a completely false view. For these things will not fail to materialize; they will come about. What is important is whether they are introduced into the course of world history by human beings who have selfless knowledge of the great goals of earthly evolution. The issue is whether those who introduce these things do so for the salvation of humanity, or whether they are brought onto the scene by groups of human beings who only exploit these things for egotistical or group-egotistical purposes. It is not what is coming that matters in this case, as what is coming is coming for certain; it is how these things are dealt with that matters. What is coming is simply what is in accordance with the Earth's evolution. The forging together of human nature with the nature of the machine will be a significant problem for the rest of the Earth's evolution.

I have frequently pointed out, quite deliberately, including in public lectures,[51] that human consciousness is associated with forces of destruction. Twice I have said in public lectures in Basel: into our nervous system we die. These forces, these death forces, will become ever more powerful. And the connection will be made between the death forces in the human being, which are related to electromagnetic forces, and outer machine forces. In a sense, the human being will be able to let his thoughts flow into the machine forces. As yet undiscovered forces within the human being will be discovered, forces that have an effect on outer electrical and magnetic forces.

That is the first problem: the merging of the human being with what is mechanical, which must become ever more pronounced in future.[52] The second problem lies in an area of life that will draw on spiritual relationships for assistance. It will only be possible for this to be done, however, when the time comes and there are sufficiently many people prepared in the right way. But spiritual forces must be mobilized in order to provide human beings with a mastery over life in relation to illness and death.

The science of medicine will become spiritualized, highly, highly spiritualized. Of all these things, caricatures are being created by certain groups, which, although they are only caricatures, indicate what really has to come about. Again, the issue with this problem is that those same groups, whom I just referred to in relation to the other problem, intend to approach it in an outer egotistical or group-egotistical manner.

The third problem concerns the introduction of human thoughts into the coming-into-being, into the birth and conception, of human beings themselves. I have pointed out that there have already been congresses held on this matter, and that there are even attempts to justify the development of a materialistic science of procreation and the union of male and female. All these things point to something highly significant that is in the process of becoming a reality. Today, one can still make the cheap point of asking why those who properly understand these things do not apply them. In future, it will be apparent to people what is involved in such a practical application, and which forces are at work, for example, in hindering the development of a more comprehensive spiritualized medicine or spiritualized economy. At present, one cannot do more than talk about these things until such time as human beings will have understood them sufficiently well in order to take them up in a selfless fashion. Many believe that they are able to do this today, that they can achieve this by themselves. There are, however, still many factors of life that can only be overcome in the correct way if, first, an opportunity can be found for an ever deeper understanding, and provided one deliberately abstains, for some time at least, from a direct large-scale practical implementation.

These things have all developed in such a way that, it is fair to say, little has remained of what, up until the fourteenth and fifteenth centuries, still lay behind the old atavistic endeavours. Today, people often talk about the old science of alchemy (sometimes one is even reminded of the process for creating a homunculus, and so on), but what is said about it is mostly incorrect. When, one day, people are able to understand what can be said about the homunculus scene in Goethe's *Faust*, then they will be better informed about these things. But the fact is that from the sixteenth century onwards these things have been shrouded in mist and have faded from human consciousness.

The law that determined this situation is the very same law that governs the rhythmic transition from waking to sleeping in human beings. Just as human beings are little capable of defying sleep, just as little capable was humanity of preventing itself from sleeping through spiritual science in relation to its spiritual development, which is what characterizes the centuries since the sixteenth century. It was necessary for humanity to sleep through spiritual life for a while, in order for spirituality to arise in a new form. These kind of necessities need to be understood; but we must also not let ourselves be depressed by them. Instead, we need to be all the more clear that the time for awakening has now arrived. We must participate in this awakening, as many events are running ahead of our knowledge. If we cannot bring ourselves to acquire this knowledge, we will not understand the events happening around us.

I have now pointed out to you a few times that certain occult groups are in pursuit of the egotistical aims that I have repeatedly indicated in these discussions. For a time, it was necessary that a certain area of knowledge was forgotten by human beings—an area of knowledge that today is often labelled with words such as 'alchemy', 'astrology' and so on, which are not understood. A certain area of knowledge was forgotten so that human beings no longer had the possibility of deriving soul content from their observations of the natural world, but instead had to rely on themselves to a greater extent. And in order to awaken forces inside themselves it was necessary that certain things took place in an abstract form, which now have to assume a concrete spiritual shape.

Three ideas have gradually formed over the course of the past few centuries that, in the manner in which they have come among human beings, are abstract ideas. While Kant named them incorrectly, they were correctly named by Goethe.[53] Kant called these three ideas: 'God, freedom and immortality'. Goethe correctly called them: 'God, virtue and immortality'.

What lies behind these things is indeed the same as what human beings today view more abstractly, and what, up until the fourteenth and fifteenth centuries, were viewed more concretely, but which, in the old atavistic sense, were also meant more materially. In those times, people experimented in the old manner by attempting to observe in alchemical experiments the processes that would show the unfolding activity of God. The aim was to create the Philosopher's Stone.

There is something concrete behind all of these things. The Philosopher's Stone was to give human beings the possibility of becoming virtuous, although this was thought of more in a material sense. It was also meant to enable human beings to experience immortality, to place themselves in a certain relationship with the cosmos, so that they could experience within themselves what extends beyond birth and death. All the washed out ideas with which one today seeks to understand these old things no longer correspond to what was intended back then. Matters have become abstract, and modern humanity speaks in terms of abstract ideas. It has attempted to understand God through abstract theology, and virtue also as something purely abstract. The more abstract, the more modern humanity is willing to speak about these things. The same applies to immortality; one speculates about what it is in the human being that might be immortal. In the first Basel lecture,[54] I spoke of today's philosophical science, which occupies itself with questions such as immortality. In this regard, I said that it is a famished, an undernourished science, which is just another way of expressing the abstraction that is sought in pursuing these questions.

In certain brotherhoods of the West, however, people have maintained a connection with the old traditions and are endeavouring to use this connection in the relevant way in order to place it in the service of group egoism. It is necessary that these things get pointed out. Naturally, if such matters are discussed by this quarter in the West in public exoteric literature, then God, virtue (or freedom) and immortality will also be spoken about in an abstract way. It is only known within circles of initiates that this is all just speculation, that these are all abstractions. For themselves, these initiates seek something much more concrete with these abstract notions of God, virtue and immortality. And that is why these words are translated for the initiates in the relevant schools. 'God' is translated as 'gold', and one seeks to discover the secret that could be called the secret of gold. This is because gold, the representative of what is Sunlike within the Earth's crust, does indeed contain a significant secret within itself. Materially, gold is related to other substances in the same way as, within the realm of thought, the concept of God is related to other thoughts. But what matters is how this secret is understood.

And connected with this is the group-egoistic exploitation of the mystery of birth. The goal here is to acquire a truly cosmic understanding. In the modern period, human beings have supplanted this cosmic understanding with an understanding that is purely telluric. If people today wish to examine, for example, how the germ of life develops in animals or human beings, they examine with their microscope what exists in the particular spot in the world on which they have trained their microscope. This is what they believe one needs to examine. But that cannot be what is of consequence. People will discover (and certain circles are close to discovering) that what acts as a force is not contained within what one views under the microscope, but enters from the cosmos, from the constellation in the cosmos. If a germ of life is created, then it is created in such a way that, within the organism in which the germ of life is formed, forces from all directions of the cosmos, cosmic forces, are at work. And if fertilization occurs, what results from the fertilization is determined by the cosmic forces that were active during the fertilization.

People will realize something that today is not yet understood. Suppose there is an organism, let us say, a hen. When a new germ of life is created within this organism, the biologist examines how an egg is developed out of this hen, so to speak. He examines the forces within the hen itself that enable the egg to develop. That is a nonsense. The egg does not develop out of the hen; the hen merely provides the substrate. Forces work out of the cosmos to bring forth the egg on the ground that is prepared in the hen. Today's microscope-wielding biologist believes that what he sees under his microscope, his microscopic field of view, is also where the forces are that matter. But what he sees there depends on the forces of the stars, which work together at a particular point within a certain constellation. The truth, the reality, will only be discovered when one discovers the cosmic nature of what is at work; it is the cosmos that conjures the egg into the hen.

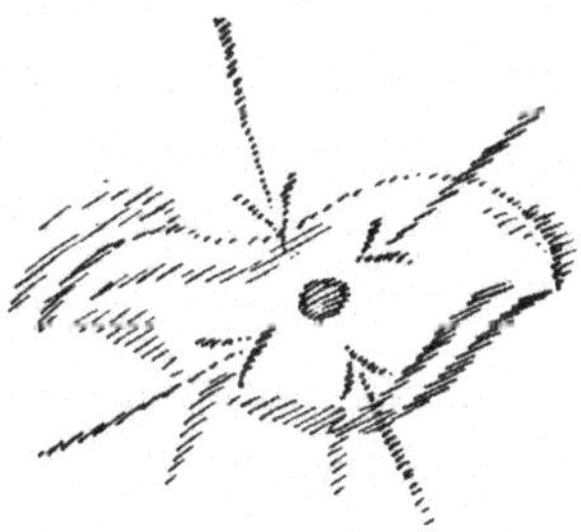

Fig. 6

All of this is connected, first and foremost, with the mystery of the Sun, or, seen from the earthly point of view, with the mystery of gold. Today, I am giving a kind of indication of the programme of what is to come in the future; these things will become much clearer to us in the course of time.

Virtue is not called 'virtue' in these schools that we are

talking about, but is instead simply called 'health'. The aim in these schools is to identify the cosmic constellations connected with the human processes of healing and falling ill. By becoming familiar with cosmic constellations, one discovers the individual substances that are in the Earth's surface, the vital fluids, and so on, which, in turn, are connected with states of health and sickness. From a certain quarter, an ever more material form of medical science will be developed, which will rest, however, on a spiritual basis.

An opinion will be spread from this quarter that human beings cannot become morally good through the abstract learning of all sorts of ethical principles. Instead, it will be claimed that human beings can become morally good by ingesting, let us say, copper under a certain constellation, or arsenic under another constellation. You can imagine how human beings of a group-egotistical persuasion might exploit these things in the pursuit of power! One only has to withhold this knowledge from others, who then cannot take part in it, and one has the best means of controlling great masses of people. One does not even have to talk about these things; one could simply introduce some kind of new delicacy, for example. For this new delicacy, which will have been manipulated in the relevant way, one then just needs to find some sales streams and ensure the necessary steps are taken, assuming one views these things materialistically. One has to be aware, however, that, in all material things, there are spiritual forces. Only those who know that, in a true sense, there is nothing material but only spiritual are able to discover the secrets of life.

The same applies to the efforts from this quarter to bring the problem of immortality into the materialistic stream. This problem of immortality can be brought into the materialistic stream in the same way by exploiting cosmic constellations. What is then achieved is not what is often speculated to be immortality, but a different kind of immortality. As it is not yet possible to extend life by influencing the body by artificial means, one prepares oneself by undergoing experiences with one's soul that enable one, after death, to remain in some lodge of brothers, and to collaborate there by drawing on forces that are available to one after death. Immortality in these circles is therefore simply called 'the extension of life'.

Of all these things you see the outward signs, of course. I do not know if there are any among you who noticed the book that caused a sensation for a while, which also came over from the West, and which was entitled *Der Unfug des Sterbens* [The Nuisance of Dying].[55] These things all tend to run in that direction, but they are just the beginnings, for what has progressed further than a beginning remains very closely guarded as an esoteric matter for the sake of group egoism. However, these things are indeed possible if they are brought into the materialistic stream, if one turns abstract ideas of God, virtue and immortality into concrete ideas of gold, health and the extension of life, if one exploits what I presented to you as the great problems of the fifth post-Atlantean period in a group-egotistical sense. What the Professor and Doctor of Theology and Doctor of Philosophy refers to by the nebulous term 'cosmic feeling' is already being widely presented to people (and unfortunately by many in an egoistic sense) as cosmic knowledge. For centuries, science has only considered what operates side-by-side on Earth, and has eschewed looking up to what comes from beyond the Earth, from beyond the telluric, as the most significant influences. In the fifth post-Atlantean period, it is these very forces that enter from the cosmos that will be put to use. For the ordinary professor of biology today, it is important to have a microscope that is capable of enlarging things as much as possible and to have the most accurate laboratory procedures, and so on. In future, when science will have been spiritualized, it will be just as important whether one carries out certain processes in the morning, in the evening or at midday; whether one lets what one did in the morning be, in some way, further worked upon by the influences of the evening, or if one excludes and paralyses the cosmic influence between morning and evening. These kinds of processes will prove necessary in future; they will be put into practice in future. Of course, much water will have flown down the Rhine before the purely materialistically oriented university chairs, laboratories, and so on, have been handed over to spiritual scientists. However, they will have to be handed over if humanity does not wish to succumb entirely to decadence. Laboratory work will have to be replaced with the kind of work that, for example, will be necessary to do good in the near future. This work will be carried out in such a way that certain processes take place in the morning and are then adjourned for the rest of the day, so that the cosmic stream passes through them again in the evening and rhythmically takes into custody what was achieved that day until the following morning. Processes will thus always run in such a way that certain cosmic effects during the day are interrupted, and that the cosmic morning process and evening process are introduced. To that end, a whole variety of new social arrangements will be required.

It will be clear to you from this that, if one is not in a position to collaborate publicly in these things, one can merely talk about them. The same quarter that intends to place gold, health and the extension of life in place of God, virtue and immortality is attempting to exclude working with morning and evening processes in favour of something else entirely. I pointed out to you last time that, on the one hand, the aim is to remove the impulse of the Mystery of Golgotha from the world by introducing another impulse from the West, a kind of Antichrist. From the East, meanwhile, the Christ impulse as it emerges in the twentieth century is to be paralysed by diverting attention and interest away from the appearance of the Christ in the etheric.

Those in the West who will seek to introduce the Antichrist as the Christ are attempting to exploit what is able to act within the most material of forces but which, in actual fact, acts through the most material of forces with a spiritual effect. Above all, this quarter is seeking to exploit electricity and, in particular, the Earth's magnetism in order to generate effects that will affect the whole of the world. I have explained to you how the Earth's forces arise in what I have called the human doppelgänger. This is a secret that will be discovered. It will be an American secret of how to use the double nature of the Earth's magnetism, with its north and south magnetic poles, in order to send controlling forces throughout the world that will have a spiritual affect. Have a look at the map of the Earth's magnetism and compare it with the following: the direction of the magnetic needle, where it swings to the east or west, and where it does not show a swing. I cannot give you anything more than indications of these things, but there are spiritual beings who continuously act from a certain compass direction. One only has to place these spiritual beings into the service of earthly existence to discover the secret of the Earth's magnetism (because these beings, who bring in their influences from the cosmos, are able to reveal this secret). In relation to gold, health and the extension of life, one will then be able to achieve a very significant group-egoistic effect. It will simply be a matter of finding the questionable courage to undertake these things, which, within certain circles, will certainly be found!

In the East, it will be a matter of strengthening what I have already discussed, by placing beings who stream in and act from the other side of the cosmos into the service of earthly existence. A great battle will ensue in the future. The science of mankind will extend into the cosmic realm, but there will be different ways in which the science of mankind will seek to make inroads into the cosmic realm. It will be the task of the good, salutary science to find cosmic forces that can be generated on Earth by bringing together two cosmic streams flowing in different directions. These two cosmic streams will be Pisces and Virgo. Most importantly, the secret will have to be discovered of how, out of the cosmos, Sun forces act from the direction of Pisces, which combine themselves with what acts from the direction of Virgo. This discovery will be a discovery for the good: how forces from two sides of the cosmos, morning and evening forces from the directions of Pisces and Virgo respectively, can be placed in the service of humanity.

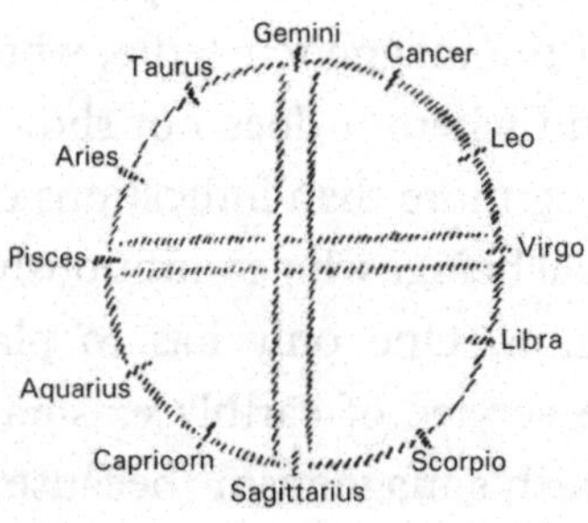

Fig. 7

These forces will be ignored by those [brotherhoods] who will attempt to achieve everything through the dualism of polarity, through negative and positive forces. With the help of the dual forces of magnetism, the positive and the negative, spiritual secrets enable spiritual content to stream out of the cosmos through the Earth from the direction of Gemini; they are midday forces. Today, it is known exoterically by scientists that, behind the constellation of Gemini in the zodiac, there is some kind of positive and negative magnetism, which even in ancient times was known to be something that is of a cosmic nature. The aim of those brotherhoods will be to paralyse what can be gained from out of the cosmos through the revelation of duality, to paralyse it in a materialistic-egoistic way through the forces that stream towards humanity particularly from the direction of Gemini, and which can be placed entirely in the service of the doppelgänger.

In the case of the other brotherhoods, those who wish above all to bypass the Mystery of Golgotha, it will be about exploiting the twofold nature of human beings. This twofold nature, which, as human beings have entered the fifth post-Atlantean period, contains human nature on the one hand and the lower animal nature on the other. In a sense, the human being is really a centaur; he contains the lower animal nature in his astral being, while his human nature is merely superimposed, in a sense, on this animal nature. The working together of the two aspects in the human being also results in a dualism of forces. This is the duality of forces that will be used by certain egoistic brotherhoods, mainly eastern, Indian groups, in order to mislead the European East, which has the task of preparing for the sixth post-Atlantean period. This dualism draws on forces that act from the direction of Sagittarius.

In the future, humanity will be faced with either conquering the cosmos for itself in two false ways or in the one right way. There will be a real renewal of astrology, which in its old form was atavistic, and which cannot continue in this old form. Those who have knowledge of the cosmos will battle against each other. Some will apply the morning and evening processes in the manner I indicated. In the West, meanwhile, the morning and evening processes will be excluded by those with a preference for the midday processes, and, in the East, by those with a preference for the midnight processes. Substances will no longer be manufactured based on the chemical forces of attraction and repulsion, because one will know that a different substance is produced depending on whether one uses the morning and evening processes, or whether one uses the midday or midnight processes. One will know that these substances have completely different effects on the trinity of God, virtue and immortality (on gold, health and the extension of life). Out of the interaction of what comes from Pisces and from Virgo it will not be possible for anything unrighteous to be brought about. What will be achieved will be the separation of the mechanism of life from the human being without establishing any power or control of one group over others. The cosmic forces that will be drawn upon from this direction will generate strange machines, which will only be of the sort that will take over the work of human beings because they will contain within them a certain force of intelligence. Large temptations will emanate from these machine-animals produced by people themselves, and it will be the task of a spiritual science that explores the cosmos to ensure all these temptations do not exert any damaging influence on human beings.

However, it must be said in relation to all of this that it is necessary that human beings prepare themselves. They can no longer take realities for illusions, but must truly acquire a spiritual conception of the world, a spiritual understanding. So much depends on seeing things for what they are! But one can only see them for what they are if one is able to apply the concepts and ideas that derive from anthroposophically oriented spiritual science to become reality. To a large degree, it will be the dead who will collaborate with us for the rest of earthly existence, and how they contribute will be what matters most. Above all, the way human beings behave on Earth will result in a large distinction between the directions taken by the contributions of the dead. On the one hand, the collaboration of the dead will be guided in a good direction, where the dead can act out of their own impulses from the spiritual world, which the dead experience *post mortem*.

In opposition to this, many efforts will be undertaken to introduce the dead into human life by artificial means. Indirectly, via Gemini, the dead will be introduced into human life in such a way that human vibrations will continue to resonate, continue to vibrate, in the mechanistic processes of the machine. The cosmos will bring machines into movement via the indirect route that I just indicated.

When these problems arise, it will be important that one only uses those elemental forces that belong to nature anyway; that one does not introduce unsuited forces into the realm of life subjected to these machines. In the occult sphere, one will have to refuse to harness human beings themselves to the mechanism in a way that applies the Darwinian theory of selection to the labour productivity of human beings, as I described in the example I gave yesterday.

I am giving all these indications, which cannot exhaust all there is to say about this subject in such a short time, because

I believe you will meditate further on these matters and will attempt to link them to your own life experiences, especially those life experiences that are gained in these difficult times. You will see how many things become clear to you when you consider them in the light that can be provided by these ideas. For, truly, what matters in our time is not the opposition of the world powers and power constellations that one frequently speaks about in outer, exoteric life, but other things entirely. At present there is indeed a kind of veil spread out over the real impulses, which are what matter. Certainly, there are particular human forces at work that are seeking to salvage something for themselves. What is there to be salvaged? Certain human forces are at work promoting the impulses that were justified impulses up until the French Revolution, and which were represented by certain occult schools. They are being promoted in a retrogressive ahrimanic and luciferic fashion in an attempt to preserve the kind of social order that humanity believed it had overcome for good at the end of the eighteenth century.

In the main, there are two powers that oppose one another: the representative of the principle that was overcome at the end of the eighteenth century and the representative of the modern age. Naturally and instinctively, a large number of people are representatives of the impulses of the modern age. That is why those who are required to be representatives of the old impulses—of the eighteenth, seventeenth and sixteenth centuries—need to be bound by artificial means to the forces that emanate from certain brotherhoods that are working to achieve group-egoistic aims. The most effective principle of the modern period that can be used to extend power over as many human beings as one needs is the economic principle, the principle of economic dependency. But this is merely a means to an end. What is at stake is something entirely different. From all the indications I have given you, you will realize what is at stake. The economic principle is connected with all that can be used to assemble a large number of people all over the Earth into an army, as it were, for these principles.

These are the things that oppose one another; what I have just pointed out to you is really what is currently at war with each other in the world. The principle of the eighteenth, seventeenth and sixteenth centuries embedded in the West, which goes unnoticed because it is clothed in the phrases of revolution and in the phrases of democracy, assumes this mask in order to achieve its aim of acquiring as much power as possible. It is advantageous for these aims if as many people as possible do not seek to examine how matters really stand, but let themselves be lulled by Maya, again and again, the Maya which one could express with the words: there is a war at present between the Entente and the Central Powers.

That war does not exist in reality; what is at stake are entirely other matters, which are the true realities behind this Maya. The former, the war of the Entente with the Central Powers, is just Maya, just the illusion. What is at war with one another can be seen by looking behind the things, by illuminating them in the way that, for certain reasons, I have only indicated today. For oneself, at least, one must strive not to mistake illusions for realities. That way, gradually, the illusion will be dissolved, as far as it needs to be dissolved. Today, most of all, one must try to see matters in the way that they present themselves to an unprejudiced sense for reality.

AFTERWORD

by Andreas Neider

After the reader has let the content of the foregoing lectures by Rudolf Steiner sink in, questions will have arisen. Perhaps much that was said in these lectures will have remained difficult to comprehend, or possibly even disquieting, despite the editor's efforts to shed some light in the introductory comments.

Let us return, therefore, to the fundamental thought that was set out in the Introduction. Our inner life and our focused attention, i.e. our astral body and our 'I', are not located within our physical body, but outside of it, in the periphery; our physical body merely serves as a mirror for this inner experiencing. With the help of the life forces that have been transformed into thought forces, the etheric body conveys inner experiences, via the cerebrospinal fluid and our breathing, to the nervous system, the brain, which forms the actual mirror. All of this was set out in the Introduction. However, let us look again more closely at the nervous system, in which, as Rudolf Steiner said in the lectures, there lives a doppelgänger who finds his expression in our electrophysiology. During the course of the twentieth century, this electrophysiology was carried over to the world of machines, to the computer. But what does it mean for this aspect of the human being to be transferred to machines, where it now acts as an 'electronic doppelgänger'?

Rudolf Steiner spoke elsewhere about our nervous system, and we can draw on the comments he made there to help us:

This nerve apparatus sends out its branches to our outer surface areas, and then back into our interior, where, as in the surface, the nerve endings dissipate again. Between these two are the middle zones, which include the brain and, in particular, the spinal and ventral nerve cords. This is where we are able to be really quite awake; we are most awake where the nerves are most developed. But the nervous system has a peculiar relationship with the spirit. It is a system of organs, which, as a result of the functions of the body, has a continual tendency to decay, to become mineral in nature. If it were possible to isolate the nervous system of a living person from the rest of his bodily being, from the glands, muscles, blood and bones (you could even keep the skeletal system with the nervous system), then, within the living human being, this nervous system would already be a corpselike element, a perpetual corpse. The perpetual death of the human being takes place within the nervous system. The nervous system is the only system that does not have any direct relationship with the soul/spirit. Blood, muscles, and so on, always have a direct relationship with the soul/spirit, whereas the nervous system has no direct relationship at all. The nervous system only has a relationship with the soul/spirit in that it continually excludes itself from the human organism. The nervous system is not present because it is continually in a state of decay. The other members of the human being are alive; they therefore form direct relationships with the soul/spirit. The nervous system is continually dying off. It continually tells the human being: you are only able to develop yourself because I do not present you with any obstacles; I make sure that I am not present in any way

> with my life. That is what is peculiar. In psychology and physiology you will find the nervous system portrayed as the mediating organ for our sensing, our thinking and our soul/spiritual life as a whole. But in what way is it able to act as this mediating organ? It is only able to do so by perpetually excluding itself from our life, by not creating any obstacles for our thinking and feeling. In other words, it does not establish any connections with our thinking and feeling. Where it is located, it leaves the human being empty with regard to the soul/spirit. Where the nerves are located, there are just empty spaces for the soul/spirit. Where there are these empty spaces, the soul/spirit is therefore able to enter.[56]

And, at another point:

> Although people have moved away from this position to some degree these days, it was not so long ago that one based everything on electrical currents and the like. However, when it comes to electrical currents, what we are actually dealing with (I am about to tell you something that derives solely from higher knowledge) is not a 'flowing-into of something'. In truth (if I can indicate this schematically here with a wire, through which the so-called electrical current is meant to flow), what we are dealing with is an empty space in [the fabric of] reality.
>
> If I referred to reality as '+a' (I am now speaking of a degree of reality, which is something that many people would not be prepared to countenance), then I would have to refer to the reality that exists within the wire as '−a'. And so we have a 'sucking in' of what is otherwise always considered to be a 'flowing into'. In essence,

> what we are dealing with is an electrical conductor, which therefore does not take up space, but is an empty space in spiritual terms. And this leads us on to the nature of the will, which was only presaged here by Dr Stein.[57] In reality, the nature of the will has nothing to do with, for example, our nerves. Our nerves take up space, but what we are dealing with in relation to the will is the empty space within the hollow channels and tubes, through which the spirit is drawn in, through which it passes.[58]

From a spiritual point of view, our nerves are therefore hollow spaces in which no organic life exists, and in which, for that reason, the spirit can be reflected.

So when we consider the transfer of this aspect of the human being to the computer, then, from a spiritual perspective, we are dealing with hollow spaces, which, as Steiner explains, have a suction effect. But is the human 'I' able to occupy these hollow spaces?

To answer that question, let us consider the relationship between the body and the soul. If my 'I' attaches itself to something through the focused attention of my thinking, then my astral body is able to occupy the whole of that something with soul. The soul's experiencing is then reflected in the physical body with the help of the 'free forces' provided by the etheric body. The latter bring the soul/spiritual experience as images before our minds, which, in turn, can be assimilated by the nervous system. If our attention is then focused elsewhere, after the soul experience has ended, the mental images created by the etheric body are retained as memories and can be called back to life later. That is how the soul/spirit lives within the body.[59]

Now, what takes place in the case of the computer? Let us first consider a traditional PC, which has not been networked, but merely serves as a tool for writing, or for storing photographs or other data. The hollow spaces of the computer can continue to serve as a mirror for the intentions of the 'I', for what is experienced by the astral body, whether as records of our thoughts, digital photographs, spreadsheet calculations or other data.

However, even in the case of digital photographs, the data begin to detach themselves from the 'I'. In the case of analogue photography, the film materials that were used provided a natural limit for the number of pictures that could be taken, which were also limited for financial reasons. A role of film with 36 pictures was worth money, which one did not want to waste unnecessarily. Every photograph therefore had a real financial value. If you developed your photographs yourself, then every picture became something valuable. The 'I' remained attached, as it were, with every picture. This is no longer the case for digital photography. Storage capabilities today are almost unlimited, while developing photographs has been replaced by digital processing. Although it is still possible for the 'I' to unite itself with every picture, this is not what actually happens. As every mobile phone today is also a camera, ever more photos are taken with which no conscious attention, no 'I' is connected.

Technical progress has now gone a step further by networking individual computers in a similar way to the way in which our nerve cells are networked in the brain. Let us have another look, therefore, at our nervous system. Here, there are also areas that are not occupied by our soul/spirit, such as our reflexes, where the nervous system reacts autonomously, without our presence in soul/spirit. Lightning-fast reflexes are present everywhere in the virtual world of the internet, where connections and links are constantly being made that are not permeated by human consciousness. The internet thus enables the emergence of an independent form of intelligence that can act all around the Earth in a flash, and is no longer controlled by human beings, but by machines. For example, with the help of this intelligence, a large proportion of those emails are generated that we call spam. Most transactions in the speculative financial economy are also carried out by networks of computers and computer programs. At the same time, everything a user of the internet does is recorded somewhere on the web, and can be used by programs to create future links.

This kind of anonymous spirit has been expanding rapidly over the past decade or so. Human identity and 'I'-attentiveness are lost in favour of anonymous shadows.

In addition, we have what are known as avatars, the aliases assumed by internet users. Furthermore, there are ever greater volumes of data, images, videos and music clips being uploaded to the web, which form a growing mass of 'I'-less, soulless content, for which the electricity that powers the internet serves as a basis. It is also apparent from the ever greater threat to copyright and the systematic violation of personality rights on the internet that what we are dealing with here is an expunging of the ego.

The nervous system has been replaced by digital technology, while the 'free forces' of the etheric body have been replaced by the interconnectivity of computers. But what is it that replaces the soul/spirit? What kind of spirituality occupies the ever more widespread anonymity of the internet? On what kind of spirituality does the internet have a suction effect, provided it is no longer occupied by conscious human attention?

At this point, we can consider again some of the statements made by Steiner in the foregoing lectures:

> If these brotherhoods then make arrangements for these souls to come into the domain of their brotherhood after death (a feat that quite probably lies within their nefarious power), then the power of such a brotherhood will thereby be increased immensely. These materialists are therefore not materialists because they deny the existence of the spirit—they are not that foolish, these materialist initiates, for they know the truth about the spirit very well. They do, however, bring it about that souls remain within the material realm after death, so that the brotherhoods are then able to make use of them for their own purposes. In other words, these brotherhoods establish a clientele consisting of the souls of the dead who remain in the earthly realm. The souls of the dead have within them forces that can be directed in many different ways to achieve various effects. By these means, one is able to exert very special kinds of power over those who are not initiated into these things.[60]

> To a large degree, it will be the dead who will collaborate with us for the rest of earthly existence, and *how* they contribute will be what matters most. Above all, the way human beings behave on Earth will result in a large distinction between the directions taken by the contributions of the dead. On the one hand, the collaboration of the dead will be guided in a good direction, where the dead can act out of their own impulses from

> the spiritual world, which the dead experience *post mortem*.
>
> In opposition to this, many efforts will be undertaken to introduce the dead into human life by artificial means. Indirectly, via Gemini,[61] the dead will be introduced into human life in such a way that human vibrations will continue to resonate, continue to vibrate, in the mechanistic processes of the machine. The cosmos will bring machines into movement via the indirect route that I just indicated.[62]

In answer to the question of what kind of spirituality can act within the electronic doppelgängers and, in particular, within the internet, the above statements by Steiner at least suggest the following hypothesis: in so far as electronic media are copies of our nervous system, and therefore constitute empty spiritual spaces, they could attract the spirituality of those souls who have been unable to release themselves from material existence after death.

The fixation on the material realm mentioned by Steiner in the lectures should be seen in close connection with the 'fall of the spirits of darkness', which Rudolf Steiner discusses again and again in this context. Without human opposition, the 'spirits of darkness' will bring about an ever greater fixation on the purely material realm. This can also be expressed as an ever greater fixation on mirror images of our nervous system, which is what computer networks are: mirror images, doppelgänger-like copies of our nervous system.

One could easily dismiss this kind of hypothesis as wild speculation if there were not, especially within the media themselves, hidden indications of what has been suggested here. Mention should be made of one of the most well-known examples, *The Lord of the Rings* by J.R.R. Tolkien. Tolkien places the symbol of the ring at the centre of his attempt to create a new mythology.[63] The ring is a symbol of materialism (as was also the case with Richard Wagner), a symbol of the ever greater fixation of human beings on the material. And the Lord of the Rings is none other than Ahriman, whom Tolkien calls 'Sauron'. Now, Sauron has powerful assistants, the *Nazgûl*, the *spirits of the Ring*, who are pertinent to what we are discussing. What are the Nazgûl? They are the dead who, during their previous lives on Earth, were fixated on one of the rings and have therefore fallen under the power of Sauron. After death, they become his slaves and are forced to act in a destructive manner.

Tolkien had acquired first-hand experience of these kinds of destructive effects in the horrific battles of attrition during the First World War. The seminal year of 1917 was also a turning point for Tolkien, who then began writing his mythology as a condemnation of materialism.[64]

Today, the destructive effects are spreading in such a way that connections between our soul/spirit and our bodily/physical nature are being broken. It is the powers of attention, above all, that are being significantly impaired, thereby denying the 'I' the possibility of connecting itself in a healthy way with the body. In place of the body, there are ever more digital devices, which, through their networking, are separated from the soul/spirit of human beings and, in this manner, provide an entry point for anonymous spirituality. Networks of computers are becoming a kind of shadow world of the spirit, without their users being conscious of this.[65]

Here is not the place to add to the many theories concerning the power of digital media. The above is merely intended as an indication of the essence of what we are actually dealing with in terms of today's digital networking.[66]

We can, however, examine a further area. What has been described so far mostly relates to our daytime consciousness and does not take into account what happens while we sleep. Here, Steiner points out that the experiences that we have during the day are imprinted into our memories at night. Physiologically this takes place by means of the 'free forces', which are at work during the day in the formation of mental images. At night, these 'free forces' stimulate, via the metabolic organism, the linking of synapses in the brain, which then recreate the experience in chronological sequence, effectively in the form of spatial structures. Connected with this are not only our conscious formation of memory pictures, but also the embedding of our memory itself to a large extent in our body, which then comes to expression in our learned physical abilities, such as our ability to write by hand, and, most importantly, in our moral behaviour.

There is, however, a further aspect connected with this holistic process of memory formation, which results from the fact that the process takes place unconsciously while we are asleep. In one of his lectures, Steiner describes how our brain is composed of several layers. Our conscious mental images live only within the uppermost layer. Our memories, on the other hand, are in a layer below, and are only accessible to our consciousness as mental images. According to Steiner, our mental images actually have a will-imbued character and are created in parallel to our conscious perceptions:

> Our ordinary consciousness actually resides in our ability to form mental images. Below this, there are certain processes that only rise to our consciousness as a

result of our ability to form mental images: our ability to form memory pictures. Below our ability to form mental images lies the actual process of perception, and only below that, our feelings. Within our head organization (or thinking organization), we are therefore able to distinguish more intimately between our ability to form mental images and our ability to gather perceptions. What we have perceived, we are then able to remember. But the underlying process remains quite unconscious; it only rises to consciousness in the form of the memory itself. What really goes on in this process within the human being is not something that he experiences. When he perceives something, he experiences the mental image. The effect of the perception is what enters into him, which, as the effect, is what enables him to recall the memory. But this process is already within the realm of the unconscious.

So, you see, it is only where we form mental images in our ordinary consciousness that we are actually human; it is only here that we are ourselves as human beings. Where we cannot reach with our ordinary consciousness (we cannot even reach to the causes of our memories), there we are not ourselves as human beings, but are integrated into the world. This is just as it is within physical life: the air you breath in, and that you now have within yourself, was outside you a moment ago; it was the world's air, now it is your air. After a short time, you return the air to the world. You are one with the world; at one moment, the air is outside you, then inside you, then outside you, then inside you. You would not be a human being if you were not connected to the world in this way. You are not just what is within your skin, as you

> are also connected with the whole of the atmosphere. Just as you are connected in this way within the physical realm, so you are also connected within the spiritual realm. The moment you enter into the next unconscious domain, the region from where memories rise up, you are connected with what we call the third hierarchy: the Angeloi, Archangeloi and Archai. Just as you are connected through your breathing with the air, so your head organization (your lower head organization, which is only covered by the outer lobes of the brain and is purely a part of the earthly sphere) is connected with what is below it, with the third hierarchy, with the Angeloi, Archangeloi and Archai.[67]

This means that the angels are involved in our formation of memory, which remains an unconscious process.

If we now look to the electronic doppelgängers, we can see that ever greater aspects of our memory formation, and therefore the formation of our abilities and our moral constitutions, are being handed over to them. The 'I' is becoming ever less aware and registers less and less of this activity. In contrast, there are ever greater volumes of data that we store on computers or on the internet in one or other of our online 'accounts' or 'profiles'.

What are the consequences of this? If our memory formation is left to the electronic doppelgänger, then the angels, the third hierarchy, can no longer play a part. The electronic doppelgänger cuts us off from the contribution of the angels to our memory formation, which takes place while we sleep.[68] The absence of this contribution also has the effect of weakening our 'I', which, as we know, has its fundamental basis in the formation of memory.[69]

In conclusion, we can say that the electronic doppelgänger is essentially taking over two consciousness processes. The first of these is the process of perception that takes place while we are awake through the conscious linking of the 'I' and the astral body with the powers of attention of the etheric body and the contents of consciousness acquired in that way. The 'I' and the astral body unite with the etheric and physical bodies in helping to maintain our focus of attention, and thereby create contents of consciousness on the basis of the formative 'free forces' of the etheric body and the nervous system.

The second process takes place while we are asleep, while the 'I' and the astral body remain unconscious. In this process, the contents of consciousness experienced by the astral body are incorporated into our memories. The etheric body works unconsciously on the physical body to create memory structures, which, likewise, depend on our nervous system as a basis.

What does Steiner mean, however, when in the last of the lectures reprinted here, he calls our attention to four processes: the midday, midnight, morning and evening processes?

> In the future, humanity will be faced with either conquering the cosmos for itself in two false ways, or in the one right way.[70]

What does that mean? In relation to consciousness technologies, this means that we are dealing with midday processes, which Steiner connects with Gemini and the polarity in electricity and magnetism, and with midnight processes, which he connects with Sagittarius, the Centaur being who is half animal, half human. The computer replaces the daytime consciousness processes (the midday process) and the processes that take place during the night (the midnight process).

This can be countered through the deliberate nurturing of the morning process (Pisces) and evening process (Virgo). In other words, through education and self-discipline, we can become aware of the transition from sleep to wakefulness (the conscious connection of the astral body with the etheric body) by tending to the sensory perception processes. Similarly, we can become conscious of the transition from wakefulness to sleep (the loosening of the astral body) by consciously tending to the formation of recollections and memories.

These are the two pillars on which all of Steiner's exercises and meditations for self-discipline rest. The fundamental principles of Waldorf pedagogy also rest on these two processes. The healthy connection of our soul/spiritual nature with our bodily/physical nature is established primarily through the strengthening of our powers of attention and powers of memory. All the exercises that Rudolf Steiner has bequeathed to us in this respect, in *Knowledge of the Higher Worlds* (GA 10), and in the lecture on *Nervousness and the 'I'*[71] (a lecture that was given a century ago) are, in essence, hygienic exercises that foster a healthy connection between the soul and the body.

As Steiner made clear in the lectures gathered here, what matters is not that we avoid or reject information technology. Instead, we need to see through and comprehend the influence associated with information technology, while also surmounting the danger of anonymization, depersonalization and the expunging of the ego:

All this does not give us any cause to lament, or anything similar, but a reason for strengthening the power and energy of the human soul's striving towards the spiritual. If human beings achieve in the fifth post-Atlantean period what can be achieved by incorporating the forces of evil in a positive sense, then something momentous will also have been accomplished at the same time [. . .] in that human souls will recognize that they have in Christ the helper they need to transform the forces of evil into good. There is one thing that is connected with this particular characteristic of the fifth post-Atlantean period, something that one should inscribe into one's soul every day anew. It is something that one should not forget, even though the human being is particularly disposed to forgetting this matter. That is, the human being in the fifth post-Atlantean period must be a fighter for the spirit; he will experience a dwindling of his forces if he does not continually control them in order to use them to conquer the spiritual world. In the fifth post-Atlantean period, the human being is left to his own freedom to the highest degree! This is something he must experience. And, in a way, everything that human beings encounter in this fifth post-Atlantean period must be measured against the idea of human freedom.[72]

NOTES

See the Bibliography of Cited Materials from the Collected Works of Rudolf Steiner for the titles of individual GA volumes.

1. The lectures are contained in GA 177.
2. Rudolf Steiner describes these matters in detail in GA 26.
3. Andreas Neider describes in *Der Mensch zwischen Über- und Unternatur* [The Human Being between Sub-nature and Super-nature], Stuttgart 2012, how images of the fall of the spirits of darkness are portrayed in today's literature for young people. One example is the novel *The Host* by Stephenie Meyer, in which a large section of humanity is possessed by aliens. Through her Twilight series of vampire novels, she has given the figure of the vampire worldwide popularity. Vampires are dead people who have not been able to extricate themselves from the earthly realm and therefore generate destructive effects.
4. Lecture of 16 November 1917, St Gallen, '*Also der Mensch kommt recht sehr* . . .', in GA 178, pp. 58 f.
5. See the lectures of 18 October 1917 and 23 November 1917, in GA 72.
6. Lecture of 25 November 1917, Dornach, '*Ich habe vollbedacht*. . .', ibid., p. 219, emphasis added by Andreas Neider.
7. John von Neumann, *The Computer and the Brain*, Yale University Press, 1956, p. 26.
8. Lecture of 16 January 1917, St Gallen, '*Und wir schreiten* . . .', in GA 178, p. 58.
9. Rudolf Steiner provides many descriptions of the nature of the luciferic doppelgänger. See the selection of texts in Andreas Neider, *Self-Knowledge: The Journey to Wisdom*, Rudolf Steiner

Press, 2015, which includes extracts from several of Steiner's basic works.

10. This fact is also addressed by phenomenological philosophy and anthropology. See Andreas Neider, *Wo steckt unser Ich?* [Where is our 'I'?], with contributions by Gernot Böhme, Thomas Fuchs and Jan Vagedes, Stuttgart, 2009.
11. See Rudolf Steiner's Bologna lecture of 1911, contained in Andreas Neider, *Das gespiegelte Ich*, Dornach, 2007. An English translation of this lecture is contained in *Seeing with the Soul: the Foundation and Scientific Validity of Anthroposophy*, Mercury Press, 1996.
12. See Andreas Neider *Das Leib-Seele-Problem oder: Wie lässt sich die 'Erklärungs-Lücke' schließen?* [The body-and-soul problem, or: How can the gap be closed?], in Issue 6/2012 of *Der Merkurstab.*
13. For an understanding of the constituent members of the human organism, see GA 9 and GA 27. Recommended further literature on the interaction of the physical body with the soul/spirit: Peter Selg, *Vom Logos menschlicher Physis* [The Logos of Human Physicality], 2nd edition, Dornach 2006; Armin J. Husemann, *The Harmony of the Human Body, Musical Principles in Human Physiology*, Floris Books, 1994; Ernst-Michael Kranich, *Der innere Mensch und sein Leib. Eine Anthropologie* [The Inner Human Being and his Body: An Anthropological Study], Stuttgart 2003; Lothar Vogel, *Der dreigliedrige Mensch* [The Threefold Human Being], 4th edition, Dornach 2005.
14. '*Diese im Ätherleibe wirksamen Kräfte ...*', in GA 27, p. 12.
15. What follows is based on the groundbreaking research by Armin J. Husemann, most recently published in *Human Hearing and the Reality of Music*, SteinerBooks, 2013. In the third chapter, 'The Experience of Music and Its Physiological Basis', Husemann sets out what Rudolf Steiner had indicated in *Riddles of the Soul* as the physiological basis of consciousness

and of the soul's experiencing in the interplay of the etheric and astral bodies. He does so in a precise manner that is easy to comprehend with the help of anatomical charts. In the present context, the physiological basis can only be briefly alluded to. For a detailed treatment, Husemann's book is highly recommended. More detailed with a view to a basic understanding of the etheric body is Husemann's standard work *The Harmony of the Human Body, Musical Principles in Human Physiology* (see note 13). On this topic, see also the comprehensive research by Peter Selg, *Vom Logos menschlicher Physis* (see note 13), in which all the passages from Rudolf Steiner's works relating to the issues addressed here are methodically and accurately set out.

16. Lecture of 29 October 1921, Dornach, '*Auf der Berührung des Atmungsrhythmus*...', in GA 208, p. 87.
17. This can be seen, as Armin Husemann shows in *Human Hearing and the Reality of Music* (see note 15), above all in the experiencing of music, which is based on the rhythm of breathing in and breathing out to an inner singing. In an ideal case, the listener breathes in exactly the same rhythm as the rhythm in which the singer or instrumentalist performs. As Husemann shows, these relationships can be investigated by way of experiment and proven very precisely. Steiner added the following to the explanatory gap under discussion: 'When a natural scientist speaks of matter existing within space, he speaks of a substance that does not yield itself up to what we use in our attempts to grasp hold of reality. For our ordinary consciousness, it remains the case that we have an inner life, which, on the one hand, does not extend as far as reality, while, on the other hand, outer reality does not yield itself up to our inner life. Between these two there is an abyss. This abyss, which one needs to be familiar with, is an obstacle for human cognition. The only way for the soul to overcome the abyss is by developing

supersensible perception, as I explained today in reference to artistic activity.

'If this faculty of perception develops, one enters into a different relationship with one's self and with the material reality that is present as the physical body. The body transforms itself into something new; it does not remain something that refuses to yield itself up to our inner life. Our inner life does not remain something that flutters above reality but impregnates itself, permeates itself, with its own bodily nature, with what has material existence in the body. But then all material existence contains spiritual existence.

'Let us try to visualize this in relation to the art of music. At the same time as human beings create musical or other mental images that they perceive in their ordinary consciousness, complicated processes take place within their bodies. People know nothing about these processes even though they are taking place. Clairvoyant consciousness penetrates into these inner, complicated, wonderful, bodily experiences. The cerebral fluid, which is otherwise embedded in the brain, flows out into the spinal cord tissue on the out-breath and pushes down, driving the blood to the veins in the lower abdomen; and, on the in-breath, everything is pushed up. A wonderful rhythm takes place that accompanies everything that we imagine and perceive. This breathing, this sculpting, pushes itself rhythmically in and out of the brain. A process takes place that contributes to human experiencing. It is something that takes place in the subconscious and the soul is aware of it. Today's physiology and biology still know almost nothing about these things; but it will become a widespread field of science.

'In earlier times, which we cannot return to now, one had to seek spiritual life in a different manner. The time for seeking spiritual science in the oriental, Indian way has passed. It can be studied in looking back, but the belief that we have to return to Indian methods is not credible. It does not offer anything for our time and would lead humanity astray. Our methods are much more intellectual, although we can still permit ourselves to study the aims of ancient Indian culture. A large part of the training for higher knowledge in Indian culture consisted of rhythmically ordering the process of breathing; its aim was to regulate the breathing process. If you compare what people were seeking for at that time with what I have just been telling you, you will find that the student of yoga wanted to experience within himself, through his inner awareness of the breathing process, what I have described. The ancient Indian became conscious of that through trying to become aware of the ebb and flow of the breathing process.

'Our methods are different. Those who seek to understand this will find that it is no longer right for us to immerse ourselves into the organism by this physical route. Instead, we should try to grasp through the meditative intellect what streams down, and, through exercises of the will, grasp what streams up. In this way, we should aim to set ourselves against the flow with our soul life and try to feel what streams up and what streams down.' Lecture of 6 May 1918, Munich, '*Wenn der Naturforscher von Materie spricht*...', in GA 271, pp. 158 f.

18. See the lecture of 26 August 1923, in GA 227.
19. Lecture of 25 November 1917, Dornach, '*Diese Kräfte, diese ersterbenden*...', in GA 178, p. 219.
20. Ibid., '*Von der Seite, wo man*...', p. 228. In this context, Steiner also points out that, by making use of electricity, the new consciousness technologies are made even stronger through additional cosmic forces out of the Gemini region of the zodiac, which are strongly associated with forces of polarization. See the Afterword.
21. Ibid., '*An solchen Stellen ist der Wille*...', pp. 218 f. In relation to the forging together of man and the machine, see the Afterword; this issue also portrayed in Rudolf Steiner's fourth Mystery Drama, where the figure of Doctor Strader speaks of

an invention that has to do with precisely this force, which, crucially, is determined by the moral consciousness of the user of this invention. The invention is described as a 'machine', without any further portrayal of what kind of mechanism it is. In the anthroposophical tradition, this invention is therefore known as the 'Strader machine' or the 'Strader apparatus'. See *Der Strader-Apparat. Modell—Skizzen—Berichte* [The Strader Apparatus. Model—Sketches—Reports] in Issue 107 of *Beiträge zur Rudolf Steiner Gesamtausgabe*, Dornach 1991.

22. '*Der Mensch muss die Stärke...*', in GA 26, pp. 257 f.
23. See Ateş Baydur, *Six Steps in Self-Development: The Supplementary Exercises*, Rudolf Steiner Press, 2010; Martina Maria Sam, *Strengthening the Will: The 'Review Exercises'*, Rudolf Steiner Press, 2010; Taja Gut, *Meditationen für den Alltag* [I am. Everyday Meditations], Rudolf Steiner Verlag, Dornach 2011; and *Breathing the Spirit: Meditations for Times of Day and Seasons of the Year*, Rudolf Steiner Press, 2007.
24. Lecture of 16 November 1916, St Gallen, '*Sie werden bemerkt haben...*', in GA 178, pp. 47–72. The last few paragraphs of the lecture refer to the day's events and have been omitted.
25. Lecture of 15 November 1917, St Gallen, in GA 178.
26. The connection between the ahrimanic and luciferic doppelgängers and illnesses has to date still been little researched in anthroposophic medicine. On the distinction between the two doppelgängers, see the Introduction by Andreas Neider.
27. Lecture of 13 November 1917, in GA 178.
28. The lecture was held in St Gallen.
29. Lecture of 6 November 1917, Zurich, '*Es gibt also...*', in GA 178, pp. 91–3.
30. At the end of the fourth Mystery Drama, *The Soul's Awakening*, Ahriman attempts to trick the initiate Benedictus through dimming the latter's consciousness, an attempt which Benedictus knows how to prevent by strengthening his conviction.

31. Lecture of 13 November 1917, Zurich, '*Ich muss in diesen Zeiten*...' (see note 27), pp. 104–10.
32. Public lecture of 12 November 1917, 'Anthroposophy and Natural Science', in GA 73.
33. Lecture of 18 November 1917, Dornach, '*Nun entsteht die Frage*', in GA 178., pp. 170–93. The first paragraph, which relates to the preceding lecture on psychoanalysis, and the last paragraph, which relates to the death of Sophie Stinde, have been omitted here.
34. In the lecture of 11 October 1915, in GA 254, Rudolf Steiner explained the designation 'Left' in more detail: 'One is on the "Left" in occultism if one pursues an ulterior aim with the help of what one espouses in occult teaching. In occultism, one is on the "Right" if one spreads the teaching for its own sake. Those on the middle path arrive at the conclusion that esoteric knowledge, which is necessary in our time for humanity as a whole, needs to be made exoteric. In contrast, those on the left-hand path are those who attach what they spread as occult teaching to special aims. One is on the "Left" to the extent that, in the pursuit of special aims, one leads human beings into the spiritual world, provides them with all sorts of revelations that are planted into them in an inappropriate manner, all merely for the purpose of realizing these special aims.'
35. See the lectures of 6 and 13 November 1917, Zurich (see note 27).
36. On the appearance of the Christ in the Etheric, cf. GA 118 and GA 130. In the first Mystery Drama, Theodora, the seeress, describes the future change in the constitution of the members of the human being as a loosening of the etheric body, which will result in the ability to perceive the Christ as an etheric being.
37. See the lecture cycle in GA 177, and also the lectures of 24 September 1916, in GA 171, and of 3 and 4 November 1917 in GA 273.

38. *Ein Faustschlag, Schauspiel in drei Akten* [The Punch, A Play in Three Acts], by Ludwig Anzengruber (1839–89). The actual German quote from Act 3, Scene 6: '*. . . so wahr ein Gott lebt!—ich bin Atheist!*' ['. . . as true as there is a living god—I am an atheist!'].
39. See the lecture of 23 September 1916, in GA 171; the lecture of 27 November 1916, in GA 172; the lecture of 26 December 1916, in GA 173, as well as the lecture cycle contained in GA 254.
40. See the lecture of 6 September 1915, in GA 163, as well as the description by Andreas Neider in *Der Mensch zwischen Über- und Unternatur* [The Human Being between Sub-Nature and Super-Nature], Stuttgart 2012.
41. See the lecture of 7 November 1917, *Anthroposophie und Geschichtswissenschaft* [Anthroposophy and History], in GA 73.
42. See note 41.
43. Lecture of 19 November 1917, '*Zunächst bitte ich Sie*', in GA 178, pp. 194–214.
44. See note 34.
45. Wilhelm Wundt (1832–1920) was a doctor, physiologist, psychologist and philosopher who, in Leipzig, established the first institute for experimental psychology. Fritz Mauthner (1849–1923) was a writer and philosopher. In Mauthner's *Wörterbuch der Philosophie Neue Beiträge zu einer Kritik der Sprache* [Dictionary of Philosophy. New Contributions to the Critique of Language], Vol. 1, p. 411, Munich/Leipzig 1910, the actual German quote is: '*So Wundt, von eines Verlegers Gnaden ein Klassiker der Philosophie*' [So Wundt, by grace of a publisher, is one of the greats of philosophy].
46. In *The Portal of Initiation* it is again the seeress Theodora who, in a karmic review, points to the Christianization of Europe by Irish monks during the period mentioned.
47. See the chapter entitled '*Die Weltanschauung der griechischen Denker*' [The World Conception of the Greek Thinkers], pp. 51–3.

48. Frederick Winslow Taylor (1856–1915) was an American engineer, originator of efficiency studies in industrial plants, and founder of scientific management (the Taylor system). See *The Principles of Scientific Management* (1912).
49. Lecture of 25 November 1917, Dornach, '*Noch einmal will ich darauf hinweisen*', GA 178, pp. 218–34. The first and last paragraphs, which again relate to issues of the day, have been omitted.
50. See the lectures of 12 November 1916, in GA 172, and of 18 December 1916, in GA 173. See also the lecture of 1 December 1918, in GA 186, and Rudolf Steiner's discussion of John Worrell Keely and the motor that Keely invented, e.g. in the lecture of 20 June 1916, in GA 169. H.P. Blavatsky also devoted a chapter of her *Secret Doctrine* to a discussion of the Keely motor. See *The Secret Doctrine, The Synthesis of Science, Religion and Philosophy* (1887–97), Vol. 1, Book 1, Part III, *The Coming Force*. See also Issue 107 of *Beiträge zur Rudolf Steiner Gesamtausgabe*, Dornach 1991.
51. See the lectures of 18 October 1917 and 23 November 1917, in GA 72.
52. In the lecture of 1 December 1918, in GA 186, Rudolf Steiner refers to the three problems mentioned here with the terms 'mechanical occultism', 'hygienic occultism' and 'eugenic occultism'. In the lecture of 9 October 1918, *The Work of the Angels in Man's Astral Body*, in GA 182, these three problems are described as aberrations of the ideals of freedom, equality and fraternity.
53. See, for instance, Immanuel Kant, *The Critique of Practical Reason*, 1788, Part 1, Book 2, Chapter VIII, 'Of Belief from a Requirement of Pure Reason': 'On the other hand, a requirement of pure practical reason is based on a duty, that of making something (the *summum bonum*) the object of my will so as to promote it with all my powers; in which case I must suppose its possibility and, consequently, also the con-

ditions necessary thereto, namely, God, freedom and immortality; since I cannot prove these by my speculative reason, although neither can I refute them' (translated by Thomas Kingsmill Abbott, University of Adelaide, 2014); Johann Wolfgang Goethe, dairy entry for September 1807, para. 7: 'What matters is that the human being continually remembers and seeks to guarantee these three ideals: God, immortality and virtue.'

54. See note 37.
55. A selection of essays by Prentice Mulford, in *The God in You* (London 1918), translated into German by Sir Galahad (pseudonym for Bertha Eckstein-Diener) as *Der Unfug des Sterbens*, Munich 1909.
56. Lecture of 28 August 1919, Stuttgart, '*Dieser Nervenappart*...', in GA 293, p. 113.
57. Walter Johannes Stein was a scientist, a pupil of Rudolf Steiner and a teacher at the first Waldorf School. As a teacher, he had asked Steiner for natural science courses for teachers, which then took place in Stuttgart in 1920 and 1921.
58. *Discussion Statement*, 8 August 1921, Dornach, '*Wenn man auch jetzt etwas davon*', in GA 320, pp. 22 f.
59. In accordance with this, Rudolf Steiner described the stages of higher knowledge as: sensory knowledge in the form of dead reflections (corresponds to the physical body), imaginative knowledge in the form of image experiences (corresponds to etheric formative forces), inspired knowledge in the form of inspirations (corresponds to the breathing of the astral body), and knowledge of essence in the form of intuitions (corresponds to the 'I').
60. Lecture of 18 November 1917, Dornach, '*Wenn diese Brüderschaften dann*...', in GA 178, p. 178.
61. Steiner connected the zodiac sign of Gemini with the quality of polarization, such as underlies the dual logic and functioning of computer technology on the basis of electricity.

62. Lecture of 25 November 1917, Dornach. '*In hohem Maße werden*...', ibid., pp. 231 f.
63. For a more detailed discussion, see Andreas Neider, *Der Mensch zwischen Über- und Unternatur* (see note 3).
64. Many people must have felt this connection unconsciously, as Tolkien was voted the author of the twentieth century in several polls at the end of the millennium.
65. Numerous contemporary novels for children and young people feature shadow worlds in which the souls of the dead who are unable to release themselves from the earthly realm are trapped. These include the Harry Potter novels. See Andreas Neider, *Der Mensch zwischen Über- und Unternatur* (see note 3).
66. In his fourth Mystery Drama, *The Soul's Awakening*, Steiner showed how the positive influence of the dead should be viewed in relation to the ever closer relationship between man and machine. This is shown in the portrayal of the relationship between Benedictus, the initiate, and Strader, the inventor and technician. Shortly before his death, Strader had developed a machine that he wanted to make available to humanity in a positive sense, i.e. without seeking power for himself. After the death of Strader, Ahriman attempts to destroy the relationship of the initiate Benedictus with the soul of the deceased Strader, but fails to do so thanks to the alertness of Benedictus. The last of the four Mystery Dramas ends with the scene (see note 21).
67. Lecture of 2 March 1924, Dornach, '*So dass eigentlich unser Tagesbewusstsein*', in GA 235, pp. 107 f.
68. Through Waldorf pedagogy, Rudolf Steiner provided a means of preventing the two negative influences described here, which are exerted during the day and at night. Waldorf pedagogy brings the soul/spiritual element together with the body in such a way that the breathing of the child is brought into harmony in a healthy way. The content of the education is approached in such a way that, during the night, the connec-

tion with the third hierarchy can be imprinted into the memory of the child in the right way. See GA 293.

69. See Andreas Neider, *Die Evolution von Gedächtnis und Erinnerung Lesen in der Akasha-Chronik* [The Evolution of Memory and Recollection. Readings in the Akashic Record], Stuttgart 2008.
70. Lecture of 25 November 1917, Dornach, '*Das Kosmische für die Menschheit*...', in GA 178, p. 230.
71. Lecture of 11 January 1912, Munich, in *Nervosität und Ichheit. Stressbewältigung von innen* [Nervousness and the 'I'. Managing stress from the inside], which includes an introduction by Frank Meyer (Dornach 2010). A similar direction is also taken by the exercises in the lecture of 18 January 1909, contained in *Die praktische Ausbildung des Denkens* [Practical Training for our Thinking] with two similar lectures and a comparative discussion by Walter Kugler (Stuttgart 2009). In relation to pedagogy, see note 68.
72. Lecture of 19 November 1917, Dornach, '*Das alles kann natürlich nicht*...', GA 178, p. 205.

BIBLIOGRAPHY

Cited Materials from the Collected Works of Rudolf Steiner

Mentioned or cited volumes of the German edition of Rudolf Steiner's Collected Works (CW) [the *Gesamtausgabe* (*GA*)], published by Rudolf Steiner Verlag, Basel, Switzerland; current English titles (various publishers) in parentheses:

Volume

9 *Theosophie. Einführung in übersinnliche Welterkenntnis und Menschenbestimmung* (2003)
Theosophy: An Introduction to the Spiritual Processes in Human Life and in the Cosmos (1994)

10 *Wie erlangt man Erkenntnisse der höheren Welten?* (1993)
How to Know Higher Worlds: A Modern Path of Initiation (1994)

14 *Vier Mysteriendramen* (1998)
Four Mystery Dramas (2015)

18 *Die Rätsel der Philosophie in ihrer Geschichte als Umriss dargestellt* (1985)
The Riddles of Philosophy (2009)

26 *Anthroposophische Leitsätze* (1998)
Anthroposophical Leading Thoughts (1998)

27 *Grundlegendes für eine Erweiterung der Heilkunst nach geisteswissenschaftlichen Erkenntnissen* (zusammen mit Ita Wegman, 1991)
Extending Practical Medicine (with Ita Wegman, 1997)

72 *Freiheit—Unsterblichkeit—Soziales Leben* (1990)
Freedom—Immortality—Social Life (not translated)

73 *Die Ergänzung heutiger Wissenschaften durch Anthroposophie* (1987)
Anthroposophy has Something to Add to Modern Sciences (2004)

118 *Das Ereignis der Christus-Erscheinung in der ätherischen Welt* (1984)
The Reappearance of Christ in the Etheric (2004)

130 *Das esoterische Christentum und die geistige Führung der Menschheit* (1995)
Esoteric Christianity and the Mission of Christian Rosenkreutz (2005)

163 *Zufall, Notwendigkeit und Vorsehung* (1986)
Chance, Providence, and Necessity (1988)

169 *Weltwesen und Ichheit* (1998)
Toward Imagination: Culture and the Individual (1990)

171 *Innere Entwicklungsimpulse der Menschheit. Goethe und die Krisis des neunzehnten Jahrhunderts* (1984)
The Inner Impulses of Evolution: The Mexican Mysteries and the Knights Templar (1984), partial translation

172 *Das Karma des Berufes des Menschen in Anknüpfung an Goethes Leben* (2002)
The Karma of Vocation (2009)

173 *Zeitgeschichtliche Betrachtungen* (2010)
The Karma of Untruthfulness, Vol. I (2005)

177 *Die spirituellen Hintergründe der äußeren Welt. Der Sturz der Geister der Finsternis* (1999)
The Fall of the Spirits of Darkness (2008)

178 *Individuelle Geistwesen und ihr Wirken in der Seele des Menschen* (1992)
Secret Brotherhoods and the Mystery of the Human Double (2004), partial translation

182 *Der Tod als Lebenswandlung* (1996)
Death as Metamorphosis of Life (2008)

186 *Die soziale Grundforderung unserer Zeit—In geänderter Zeitlage* (1990)